I0418401

Trail Talk

Life Lessons on the Sierra Trail
Volume 2

Allen Clyde

Trail Talk: Life Lessons on the Sierra Trail, Volume 2
Copyright © 2025 by Allen Clyde. All rights reserved.

Illustrations by Claudia Fletcher and Diane Breuer
Cover photographs courtesy of Allen and Deborah Clyde
Editorial and production services provided by Linden Publishing

Published by Clyde Pack Outfitters
www.dinkeystables.com

ISBN 979-8-9920457-0-3

Printed in the United States of America
on acid-free paper.

Library of Congress Cataloging-in-Publication Data on file.

This is a modern-day parable based on true events, places, and people. Many of the individuals' names have been either changed or eliminated for the sole purpose of protecting the guilty.

—Allen Clyde

White pine

CONTENTS

This book is dedicated to Claudia Fletcher.

Allen Clyde on horseback with packhorse

Preface

Pablo awoke at his usual 5:00 a.m. Nowadays this was customary, and he no longer needed an alarm clock. He felt all school year that Clyde was watching over his shoulder, and there was no escaping the early rise. This morning was different. No classes. He had taken his last final and would view his grades and transcripts on the computer. Pablo remembered what Clyde told him the day he left the high country to go to college: "Knock yourself out, do your best, for then you never have any regrets and no need to look back. Only then can you fully focus on the future. Just get the A. Even if it's an A-, remember, on your college transcript, there is no difference between an A- and an A+. It all looks the same."

As Pablo opened his computer to look up the school year's results, he was stunned to see it actually in plain text, right before his eyes. With 30 units, he had received all A's and thus a 4.0 GPA so far. At the beginning he never thought it would be possible, but he always kept in mind the slogan, "By the yard it's hard, but by the inch it's a cinch." By not associating with his old loser friends and instead fully focusing on school, he had produced the terrific results now displayed in front of him. He sat, absorbing the full impact. He was a step closer to medical school. He was actually doing it!

Closing the computer, Pablo thought how far he had come since the confused state he was in this time one year ago. His mother had come home from a doctors appointment and said, "You're going with me on the next visit. My doctor and his wife have something to discuss with you and no way are you going to miss it." Little did he know the dramatic impact that meeting was to have on his life.[1]

---

1. Read all about Pablo's first set of adventures with Clyde in *Life Lessons on the Sierra Trail*.

School was over, and he couldn't wait to start on a new summer season in the John Muir Wilderness. It was time to get packing. Clyde expected him up there at the horse packing station by this afternoon. The change of scenery was going to be another shock, since only yesterday he was sitting in class taking his last final down here in the San Joaquin Valley. It was late May but already getting hot. The 7,000 foot elevation at the station would bring welcome relief, since it was always at least twenty degrees cooler there.

Clyde had let him keep his saddle and all his gear at the station for the winter, thus he only had to pack clothes and a few books, mostly for reference. Everything he owned fit easily in the trunk of his small car. Clyde had always told him, "Don't collect crap. If you want to get far in life, travel light." Driving out of the parking lot, he noticed in his rear-view mirror the CSU Fresno sign. A smile came over him as he thought, "See ya in the fall."

Marmot

CHAPTER 1

The Trotter Effect

Pablo's left eye popped open, noticing the clock reading 4:55 a.m. Sensing the predawn light, and with his hearing coming alive, he knew Clyde was already in the corral leading out horses for the day's trip. He got out of bed and with his right hand partially opened the front door to the bunkhouse. This was the signal to Clyde that he was awake, getting up, and there was no need to holler. He had been dreaming he was back in class and was glad to be awakened into reality. This was to be the first trip of the summer season and he couldn't wait. Jumping up, it only took him minutes to get dressed, brush his teeth, and head out the door.

"Where we headed today?" Pablo asked as he approached the corral with two lead ropes in his left hand and coffee in the right.

Clyde handed him Poco, the third horse he had retrieved, and said, "Doing a food resupply for Outward Bound. They have scheduled five resupply trips so far this year. Depending on the summer, they may add a couple more. That usually depends on fires or snow problems in other areas. Got a large group today. We're taking six packhorses this trip. That usually means we are meeting up with three different groups. They all join for about two hours, get food, and head out in different directions. Some do mountain climbing, others do solo hiking, and another may do a work project for the Forest Service. We will be able to find that out once we get there."

Diamond X and Sundown were already at the hitching rail where Pablo tied up Poco. Clyde was now coming up with Pearl and Nevada. Pablo knew they only needed one more packhorse and their two riding horses. Little Shot came as the last to complete the pack string. This small Paint Horse was both a pack and saddle horse. Clyde had always said it was best to have one animal in the string that can do either duty, in case there was a problem.

Jay, Pablo's riding horse from last year, was getting old, so Clyde gave him Mesa for this season. She was young, stout, and needed more riding time. Jay was on his way to the Dinkey Creek Stables to spend the summer. The older horses usually ended up there, as it serves as a semiretirement home for the animals. They get easy jobs, like taking little kids out for an hour at a time. With only a couple trips a day, it's easy duty for these aged but still sound animals. Gives 'em a purpose and provides an introduction to the mountains for hundreds of children each year. Clyde had heard that the kids never forget their first ride on these old horses. Often they will stop back twenty and even thirty years later with the memory still fresh of the great time they had. Clyde brought this up often to Pablo. "You never know what or when an impression will be made, so just keep it all positive."

Pablo

Clyde pulled out Harley for himself. This huge black horse had done well through the winter, and had come a long way from the backyard pet he once was. He was so tall, Clyde said he could feel his ears pop every time he got on him.

Saddling up the packhorses was next. Clyde was very particular about this process. He always told Pablo that the horse's comfort was the priority. First came the regular saddle pad, then over that came a large pack pad. This pad went from low on one side, over the top, and low on the other side. It provided padding down to where the metal rings of the saddle and latigo straps came together. Keeping the rings padded and off the horse was extremely important. If this was not done, a pressure sore would be the painful result by the end of the day. Not good. The same was true for the top of the wither area. Pulling up a small amount on the top pack padding prevented the forks of the wooden pack saddle from pressing on the top of the horse's backbone at the base of its neck. The back of the pack saddle was another area to be careful. Sometimes, on a more narrow horse, a thin cross pad would be placed first, followed by the saddle pad and then finally the large pack pad. Putting too much padding wasn't good either. This resulted in the load producing too much sway back and forth on the saddle. Getting it just right for each animal's anatomy was most important. The last thing you want to do was hurt a horse or make it suffer in any way. To do so was a cardinal sin.

Putting riding saddles on the two remaining horses went smoothly. Pablo never got over how heavy Clyde's saddle was. He always carried a long saw in a scabbard, a small amount of shoeing tools, a two-way radio, water, and a whole host of small items (bug juice, extra snaps, a GPS unit, extra paperwork, etc.) distributed in his saddle bags and cantle bag behind his seat. Pablo always had trouble lifting his whole saddle rig, but Clyde flipped it up on each horse with ease. Clyde had often explained to him, "It's rarely brute strength, mostly leverage. Having the horse hold still helps too. Careful of your feet during the whole motion. A lot of people get stepped on while saddling. Just stay alert."

Loading the usual Outward Bound duffels into the pack bags went easy, even though each weighed sixty pounds. With one on each side of the horse, there were twelve loads all together.

After breakfast, the horses were loaded into the stock trailer. Stopping by the main house, where their dog Dinkey jumped in the back of the flatbed, Pablo went in and got both lunches from

Clyde's wife Deb. Driving out, Pablo could see in the rearview side mirror Deb waving, and Dinkey's nose sticking out, eager for the day's journey.

Up the Courtright Lake road they went. Pablo noticed the remaining snow patches after this season's heavy winter. Looking down onto the North Fork of the Kings River, he could see high tumbling white water and thought they were fortunate to not have to cross it on this trip. He knew even getting across Post Corral Creek, a feeder to this river, would be tricky.

Clyde, noticing Pablo's concerned look, spoke up. "That's what 1200 cubic feet per second [cfs] looks like in that river. It's been cutting loose like that for about five weeks, and this should be the last of it. I get that data from the gaging station at Meadow Brook. It sends a reading every hour to a satellite. At the beginning of spring it starts at less than 100 cfs. Then gradually works its way to 500 cfs, and then rapidly kicks up to 1200 cfs. That's when you know it's blasting, and trying to get past the river at the trail crossing would be nearly impossible and extremely dangerous.

"Back in the early 60s, a foolish packer tried to cross way downsteam at a place called Cliff Camp. Didn't want to use the bridge. He started his whole string into the raging river, only to have the whole outfit sucked downstream. He made it out alive but drowned every animal in the pack string. The Forest Service, rightly, made him get each carcass out of the river, pile wood on top, and burn 'em. Somehow he walked away without punishment. I feel, after he took care of the dead animals, they should have gotten a rope and hung him on the spot. The Post Corral Creek crossing we need to use today should be relatively easy. It's only a feeder stream and past peak flow. Outward Bound let me know by satellite phone that all got across on foot. So, I think we will be fine. But, like anything else, if we get there and it doesn't look good, don't be afraid to abort and go to plan B. One tends to live longer that way."

Continuing on the drive, Pablo noticed how different the forest was from last season at this time. A wet winter and cool spring will

4

do this. Clyde had reminded him that a straight-up average weather year is a rarity. The average is only the middle numbers between the wet and dry years. Nature works over the long haul of hundreds of years. Not minute by minute. The plants and animals have to be able to withstand the extremes in order to survive through the ages. Their resilience never ceases to amaze. Snow always seems to melt in the same pattern every year. The shady spots melt last. Also, the ones with less ground heat from rocks. The more rocky areas absorb the solar radiation and melt snow faster. That's why riding or walking around snow covered rocks is dangerous. Logs can present the same danger, but somewhat less. It's always best to have the trail memorized, like Clyde does, and know what's under any snow in the trail and make your route decision from that viewpoint.

Often Clyde had to go high on a sun-exposed hillside to get around a dangerous portion of the trail. Staying on the high and dry side has minimal impact on the land. If you need to do this, pick a different route each time to spread out and limit the imprint. Then, it's good to know where the trail is supposed to be so you can drop back down onto it when safety allows. Many people unfamiliar with the terrain have gotten lost after having to go around and not being able to find the trail again. Instead of backtracking, their ego tells them to march on, and this only worsens the problem.

Looking out the window, Pablo was surprised to see some plants growing flowers within inches of the snow melt. No time is wasted when the warm sun finally arrives. Along the road to the trailhead were many different ecosystems, from dry exposed rock areas to creek draws blasting with water. The plant life was different in each area. He remembered from looking through his reference books at night the variety of plants just in this area. There were pussy paws in the drier, gravelly areas, along with some Sierra gentian plants. Phlox plants were everywhere. Then he saw some Alpine penstemon plants, along with a bunch of penny royal. He remembered this last one was in the mint family, and when crushed had a distinct mint smell. He had heard it made a great tea when boiled.

5

Finally topping out to Courtright Lake, Pablo never got over the magnificent view of the granite domes with the wilderness backdrop. Across the dam they went and on to the spike station, where the horses were unloaded from the trailer. Loading the six packhorses, tarp and rope tying, and connecting the string only took twenty minutes. The whole process went easy, and Pablo felt good about not having lost any of the rhythm from the previous summer.

Off they went down the trail with Pablo in the lead. Going around the small snow patches was easy. The horses would be skittish in the beginning, but would soon get used to it and walk over the drifts without a second thought. Mostly the snow was hardpack, and minimal depression was made by the horses. He was careful to go around any snow that looked rotten or had water running out from underneath, signs it wouldn't hold up horses. The mosquitos were relentless. Pablo was glad for the bug juice Clyde gave him, otherwise the trip would have been miserable. Observing the snow patches in the shady areas and on north sides of the tree groups, he remembered the same from the year before. It's true, snow always seems to melt in the same pattern every year. Gaining altitude, they came through a southern exposed side of the mountain and the sun was a welcome sight and feel. Much warmer than down in the shadows.

Occasionally they would come upon a downed tree across the trail. They would stop and estimate the tree's diameter, whether it was dry or green, how much of an obstruction it presented on the trail, the amount of rerouting that was needed to get by it, and how much environmental impact the fallen tree had caused. Often Clyde would take pictures with his cellphone, especially with extremely large trees. Logging all this information and contacting the USFS trail crew leader helped prioritize the trail clearing assignments for the season. The crew would put together a game plan and start working, but often new information would come in and lead to modification of the work assignments. Other factors would play in on any decision, such as the expected amount of public travel and the impact the problems would create if the trees were not cleared soon. The point was to keep trail users on the trail and prevent collateral off-trail damage as much as possible.

What would bump a project to the front of the line would be a showstopper type problem. Often this was a large downed tree or small land slide at a critical spot in the trail where there was no option to go around, requiring the group of hikers or pack string to turn around. All this information would not only come from horsepackers, but from hikers as well. No reconnaissance data was ignored. Getting the USFS trail crews to the problem site expediently was another matter. Due to chronic short budgets, only one or at most two trail crews were ever available for the whole Sierra National Forest. Clyde always said, "Sometimes the squeaky wheel phenomenon works, so I never stop trying."

They soon came upon just one such problem. It was a twelve-inch diameter, green lodgepole pine across the trail. Even though it was a modest size tree, the location was a problem. Lying three feet above the trail and on a hard switchback, the animals could not get by without serious impact on the hillside.

Pablo stopped the string and was scratching his head when Clyde appeared at his side with a two-foot handsaw, the one he always carried in the scabbard on his saddle. He couldn't count how many times it had been needed. Handing it to Pablo, Clyde found a sunny spot on a rock and had a seat, saying simply, "I'll keep an eye on the pack string." Pablo knew this was nothing but a somewhat worthy excuse to hand the work detail off to him, as the packhorses were very unlikely to wander off.

Off to work he went, first undercutting the right side, one foot beyond the trail edge. This was the top portion of the tree suspending out beyond the trail. When he was about halfway through, he stopped and started from the top, directly above the undercut. He pounded in a small, lightweight wedge in the tip cut after his saw got partway through. The point of this was to prevent binding of the saw as the end came down with the finish cut. With this done, he moved to the left side and performed the same technique there. When that six-foot section dropped off, Pablo handed the saw back to Clyde, and then lifted the section and placed it sideways at a bend in the trail. This acted as a further guide to keep traffic on the trail. The saw itself was handled with extreme care. Clyde never let it touch the ground, especially on the tooth side. It doesn't take much for a blade to get dull, rendering the saw useless. He carefully slid it back in the leather scabbard on the right side of his horse.

Not much farther up the trail on the right side, bordering a creek at a somewhat sharp left-hand turn, was a familiar pool. Pablo noticed the same small group of tiger lilies. They were in the same place the previous summer early in the season and he felt good to see 'em again. The sun was not shining in this area yet and the plants were still closed up. They were rather nondescript, solo-stemmed, about fifteen inches tall, with only a narrow orange cup at the top representing the folded up flower. He had always thought how remarkable it was for them to close up when the sun went down and open up again during daylight. With only minor water flow, not much else was going on in the pool.

Onward they went, toward the Post Corral meadow turnoff. At this point they encountered one of the Outward Bound students being escorted out by an instructor. The instructor was carrying her backpack. The student was not limping, and had no visible bandages. Pablo stopped and politely asked, "What's up?" After sitting down, the student eagerly explained that her left knee was giving her some problems and carrying the large backpack was too much, so she was being taken out to the trailhead. Pablo glanced at her knee and saw no signs of swelling. The young hiker, about sixteen years old he guessed, saw his glance and promptly started rubbing her right knee and transformed her face to a saddened expression at the same time, glancing up at him. Pablo got the feeling this was an act, but didn't utter any words or allow his body expression to give his thoughts away. The instructor spoke up that they had a scheduled time to meet the transport vehicle and thus had to keep going. Pablo told them he understood, waved to the instructor, and said, "Maybe we'll see ya on the way back."

After about ten minutes of riding down the trail, Clyde spoke up. "Well, Pablo, what do you make of that?"

Pablo thought for a few seconds before responding. "I'm doubtful she really had any knee issues, but it was working as her ticket out of the wilderness."

"Exactly," Clyde replied. "Initially, many of these kids think an outing in the woods sounds romantic and beg their parents to send 'em on these three-week excursions. The parents happily fork out a lot of money for them to 'get tough.' The truth is, these parents should have started long before this age. I'm going to bet her parents are loving but rich and enabling. Probably helicopter parents. That young lady has probably had everything handed to her and up here that doesn't fly. Nor does it fly in adult life. Up here in the high country, it gets obvious quick which ones have the grit. You'll see the mentally unprepared kids, sitting on the side of the trail, wearing a pitiful look on their face and complaining how tough it is. I fault the parents for most of this. It's a form of arrested development that could haunt the youngster his or her whole life. I wish more parents would just let their kids go out and stub their toe once in a while and simply respond with a 'get over it' attitude. That would benefit this young generation far more that you realize.

"I have to say, though, you covered your skepticism quite well. That young lady never caught on that you thought she was a phony. That trait will serve you well in medicine. Often patients come in complaining about one issue. After examination you realize their primary complaint isn't the real issue, but you don't let on. Keep gently asking sincere questions and often the real problem will become obvious. The patient absolutely must feel you are genuinely interested in helping them before you have any chance of doing just that. Always remember, patients don't care at all about what you know until they know you care about them. I often wish medical schools would emphasize that more and not just rote memory from medicine 'cookbooks.' Anyway, keep working on maintaining a straight face until you have fully evaluated the patient. Just don't jump early to any conclusion."

Coming up to the drop-off point referred to as the Niche, Pablo led the string a good ways off the trail to lessen the impact from prior trips. This is where the food transfer would take place for the midpoint of the Outward Bound group's three-week trip.

After unloading the pack loads from the horses, Pablo noticed a strikingly beautiful lady instructor come over to greet Clyde with an old friend-type hug. Clyde was asking her about what she had been up to over the winter. Pablo didn't hear a word. Nothing could get him out of the trance of fixation he was in as he admired her beauty. She finally had to get back to work with her students. Going past Pablo, she gave him a pleasant smile because Clyde had just introduced him to her. All Pablo could do was nod his head while wearing a frozen grin on his face.

Pablo was suddenly jarred back to reality after Clyde tapped him on the shoulder and pointed to the tarps that needed folding

OUTWARD BOUND LEADER
"TROTTER"

and the lash ropes that needed to be rolled up. While performing these routine tasks, Pablo found himself drifting back to the vision of infatuation. Soon, all the empty loads were secured on the pack-horses and they were headed back down the trail.

It didn't take long for Pablo to turn in his saddle and ask Clyde the burning question. "Who was that young lady instructor and how can I get to know her? Will I see her on the next food drop run? How come I didn't see her last year? Do ya think she would go out with me after the season is over?"

Clyde could only put his head down and chuckle to himself, while Pablo looked on with a curious stare. He had always had decent luck with the ladies and felt this would be no exception. Why was Clyde getting such a kick out of this?

Finally Clyde spoke up. "Well, Pablo, I told you her go-by name is Trotter, but you didn't hear a word I said. Her real name is Rafa-elle Abramovitz. Ya, it's a mouth full, and that's why everybody calls her Trotter. And I hate to burst your fantasy bubble there, Sparky, but she is old enough to be your mother."

Pablo pulled his horse to a stop and turned it 180 degrees, thus bringing the whole string to a standstill. He just sat there staring back with a shocked look on his face.

Clyde continued, "Yep, even though without one bit of makeup, and after ten days hiking in the wilderness, she looks like a drop-dead gorgeous twenty-five year old. Actually, she's forty years old and proud of it. Also, she never gives her beauty a second thought. She's far too deep to dwell on that. Let me explain her real beauty. You probably didn't hear me ask her what she was up to this last winter. Well, Trotter started a nonprofit program down in Kenya. It's called Naretoi. It's a program supporting girls' education, women's empowerment, and local economic efforts in Maasailand, Kenya. Every winter she goes down to Africa and works with hundreds of young Maasai ladies on values and education—some of which is doing the same type of hiking treks you saw here today. She and the other leaders of that group have advanced college degrees and put 'em to good use.

"They operate a year-round boarding school that with tuition, room and board, supplies, and transportation only costs $650. That's for the whole year. Their educational outcomes are outstanding. In California, we spend over $15,000 of public money per student per year, and that's just for school. I can tell you as a school board member for over two decades, her work is most impressive. There's a lot we could learn from what she's doing down there. That brings me to another point. There are many women in this world who have outward beauty, but have far more hidden beauty inside than you can ever imagine. Deb definitely is one of those in this group. They are the group whose far greater beauty is in their hearts, principles, and will power. All you have to do is spend time to talk and most importantly listen. Find out what their focus of life is and where it's leading them. With a genuine lady of true quality, your whole world will open up to a different and grander view of beauty."

Pablo could only sit, frozen by this new revelation. Finally Clyde spoke up, "We should get going. Don't want to keep Deb waiting."

Continuing down the trail, it was hard for Pablo to keep a focus on the job at hand. No problem, Mesa was on autopilot. Looking down and forward, his vision was going up and down with the horse's head. His focus, however, was on the experience of meeting Trotter and getting her full story. He knew Clyde understood this. What else could explain his uncharacteristic silence?

On they rode for over an hour without speaking a word. Finally Clyde broke the quiet. "Pablo, right over there just past the Hobbler Lake turnoff, Deb and I found a place several years ago during hunting season where two deer and a bear had been cleaned and deboned. Actually the dog, Dinkey, brought it to my attention. What a mess. The hunters had laid out a plastic tarp to do the job. This is OK. The problem was they left it, along with used rubber gloves, paper towels with fresh blood, etc. You get the picture. She and I stopped and gathered up all the trash. It half filled one of the empty packhorses. Took almost an hour to clean it all up. Needless to say, we were both pissed. About halfway back down the trail, we encountered the hunters. They had backpacks full of meat and were quite proud. I stopped alongside of the leader and pointed for him to look inside the horse's pack bag on his side. After walking two steps over and peaking in, his eyes got wide. The silent stare on my face told him he was caught. He only looked at the other members of his group and lowered his head, knowing to try and claim it wasn't theirs would have been pointless. Because they had the meat of two deer and a bear, there was no room for the trash, he explained. I tore into him, declaring I don't care how good of hunters they are, there was no excuse for leaving this behind. I let that sink in a few seconds, then continued with telling 'em they could pick up all this trash at the trailhead, along with an introduction to the local Forest Service Law Enforcement Officer who would be waiting for them. Still, not once did they deny the deed.

"I called the LEO on the radio, briefly explained the situation, and asked him to meet me at our spike station. He was there when we arrived, took the evidence, and went over to the trailhead and was waiting for the group when they walked out to their cars. I was told later he validated their tags and handed 'em a fat ticket. Hopefully this group learned their lesson and, more importantly, passed on their experience to others. It's been forty years, and every time I see that type of disrespect to the wilderness I get irate all over again. That brings me to another point, Pablo. Whenever you are traveling as a commercial packer up here in the high country with this outfit, conduct yourself as if someone is watching everything you do from behind the trees. Go above and beyond the call of duty to leave the woods a better place. You would be surprised how other people will observe this and quietly change their habits. Most of the time you never have to say a word. But, on the rare occasion you do have to get verbal, let 'em have it hard. My feeling is, if they don't like it then don't come up and spoil it for everyone else."

Continuing down the trail, Pablo came upon the same pond with the tiger lilies. He slowed down the string to a crawl due to his amazement of what he saw. The lilies had opened up completely to catch all the rays of the sun. The flowers were a little over two inches wide, with an orange-yellow base color and spotted with purple. Also catching his eye was the pond being fully alive with small insects. Larger types skipped over the surface. He had read they might be water striders. Even though the pond was small, it was vibrant with life. He could only stop and stare at this whole small world he hadn't noticed before when the flowers were closed. From the back of the string, Clyde observed the direction of Pablo's fixation and chose not to utter a single word, just letting him soak it all in.

After several minutes, Pablo shook his head back to reality, nudged his horse to start moving, and the pack string then continued down the trail. The whole pond experience haunted him. Why was it so different now than the other times he had passed it? Maybe because this time the flowers were open and radiating a beauty over the whole small ecosystem did he slow down and take notice. He realized now it had always been there and he would have seen much more before, if he had only slowed down and looked deeper. That's when it hit him. From now on, he would call this whole phenomenon the Trotter Effect. He felt more grounded with his new revelation. Something more than silly young boy infatuation with Trotter was coming out of today's experience. The trees, grasses, small critters scampering along the trailside, all seemed to be more vibrant. Listen and look deeper was the theme. A small chickadee flashed in front of him and perched on a lodgepole branch just even with him about four feet away. He was smaller than a junco. The top and back of his head, throat, and chin were jet black. The side of his head and a small stripe above the eyes was stark white. Other than that, the whole body was gray. The sound it made revealed the obvious source of his name—*chick-a-dee*—which was sharp and high pitched.

As they continued down the trail, Pablo reflected on how much new he was learning. After the prior season he thought he had everything down pat. Now he was realizing he had just scratched the surface. Another level of his education was just getting started.

On a small curve in the trail, Pablo could easily look back and notice Clyde's reflective expression. Nothing was said for several minutes. Finally Clyde spoke up. "Well, Pablo, every day is new. There's never a shortage of opportunities to keep learning. To get the most out of each experience, never stop listening, seeing, and asking questions. Each learning experience just adds to your tool kit to handle future encounters. Don't stop making new discoveries, learning new skills, asking more questions, and, above all, listening to more points of view. All of this will help ya reach your ultimate goal, wisdom. It seems most of the young in your generation have the idea that if they just study and do well on an exam and get a degree, then that's all that matters to be a success in life. They then just focus back on the video games while laying on the couch. It's too bad they have bought into this fallacy, for nothing could be further from the truth. The ones that go through the effort to learn from different types of people are the ones who truly have the tool sets to be leaders in whatever they choose.

"Of all the millionaires and billionaires in this world that are self made, not a single one had a straight and narrow path to the top. All took dips and turns along the way. This learning curve proves over and over to be the factor that got them to the top. Taking the time to learn of all the differences in the world around you is key. Not just the plants and animals, but humans as well. You'll learn far more from focusing on those things than from any textbook. That goes for everything, from business to medicine."

Arriving back at the Courtright spike station, it didn't take long to unload the horses, get 'em into the trailer, and head back home. Only after the horses were unsaddled and walked to the corral, given ample feed, and had their water checked, did Clyde and Pablo proceed to the cookhouse for the dinner Deb had waiting.

When the dishes were cleaned, Pablo couldn't suppress a long yawn and retreated to his bunkroom. The real reason for retiring early was to get on the computer. He couldn't wait to get it powered up, click on Google, and type in the search box for Naretoi.com.

Rider chasing a bear

CHAPTER 2

Woodchuck Run

It was about 4:50 a.m. when Pablo first opened his eyes, allowing the early morning glow into his slowly awakening consciousness. Cautiously he stretched his rediscovered muscles. Mild soreness reminded him he was not yet in the shape he thought he was. By this afternoon, he would know the whole inventory of his conditioning. For now his mission was to get up, dressed, and out the door before the loud, booming voice of Clyde echoed throughout the whole station.

"Where're we headed to today?" he asked, with his left hand shielding his eyes and his right holding a newly filled coffee cup.

"We're taking a family of four up to Woodchuck Lake. The husband and wife have been with us before, but that was about fifteen years ago. Way before their kids. Now they have a ten and a twelve year old and are ready for a several night trip. Up until now, their little ones have only been on day hikes. Taking 'em out on little jaunts is a great way to break them in. Mom and Dad feel they are ready to ride in on horseback and spend a few days. Good choice of a lake for the little ones at this time of their lives. Today we'll get 'em up to a nearly 10,000-foot lake. Should be able to get 'em there around noon. It would take them two days of hard uphill walking, carrying a loaded backpack otherwise. The parents wisely waited until the young ones were this old. If they had tried this trip when the kids were six and eight, it would have been pure torture for everyone. This way the kids will love every minute of the four-hour ride. If it was longer, I guarantee the complaining would start in big time. Always best to select a destination to get all there just before with whining starts."

"Mom and Dad have done a fair amount of riding," Clyde continued, "but the young ones, never. So, let's get out Howdy and Little Shot for the kids, Jigger and Trapper for Mom and Dad. I figure three packhorses should do for their gear. Looked it over last night when they arrived. Pull out Sundown, Diamond X, and Nevada. You can ride Jay and I'll take Harley. Deb is coming too. I always prefer having her along when we have riders, especially those with kids. She wants to ride Mesa, so let's get 'em all out and saddled. One trailer can handle the ten-head load on this short drive without any trouble."

Out the gate the three went, followed by the family in their own car. Crossing Wishon Dam, they soon were at the Woodchuck trailhead. The four guest saddle horses and Deb's riding horse had been placed in the rear of the trailer, and thus were unloaded first. Leaving the packhorses and the two guide horses loaded in the trailer for the time being reduced congestion as they got everyone organized. As the clients unloaded their camping gear, Deb was setting up the saddles. She could do this with a casual glance at their body types and leg length. It was always surprising to Pablo how right on she always seemed to be when the clients mounted their horses.

With the fitting done, and the paperwork and wilderness permit completed, it was time to get the guests saddled up and on their way, led by Deb. Getting the youngest first went easy. He had perfect rhythm and hopped right up. Most impressive, because Howdy was the tallest horse we have. The oldest child, however, struggled. He would put his left foot into the stirrup, then with both hands on the saddle horn try to hoist his whole body up with just arm strength. At the end of his third failed attempt on Little Shot, he started to complain about the half step she took sideways which prevented him from getting on. Little Shot was one of our shortest horses, plus Deb was holding onto the halter.

That's when Clyde came over. Without saying a word, he motioned for the little brother to dismount and come over to his big brother's horse. Clyde then directed him to mount up on Little Shot. The smaller one did just that. After putting his left foot in the stirrup, and with both hands on the saddle horn, he bent down slightly with the right knee and hopped right up. Clyde then asked him to dismount and do it again. The older brother plus Mom and Dad were watching intently. After that Clyde turned his attention back to older brother. "Now, did ya study how he did that, most likely not even realizing all the body function involved? Don't ever try to lift yourself up with arm only strength. You can't do it for one, plus it puts one heck of a sideways pull on the saddle. Pulling the saddle over pinches the horse's back, or withers, and that is painful. Doing it slowly while you struggle up is just torture for the horse. The animal will eventually step sideways to get away from the source of the pain. You would too if the situation was in reverse. Hopping up in one swift, fluid motion is the secret. It takes core strength to put it all together. Now, let's try it again, and don't forget to hold onto the reins at the saddle horn with the same left hand. Never not have a hold of the control rein whenever you get on any horse. If you don't and the horse decides to run off, you're screwed."

Big brother then walked up to Little Shot, passing little brother, who was giving him a smart-ass grin. After placing his left foot in the stirrup, and with the left hand holding the rein and saddle horn while keeping his right hand free, he deliberately over bent his right knee and gave a mighty push off with one fluid motion. With an exaggerated bend at the waist, keeping his right hand and arm free as a balancer while the left hand and arm were used as a pivot point, he popped right up on Little Shot. The horse never moved a muscle. Big brother was just as shocked as everyone else, but quickly erased that expression off his face. He just calmly looked around and remarked, "Are you guys getting on your horses so we can leave or what?"

That said, the remaining members of group got mounted up. After Deb's safety lecture, the four guests headed up the trail with Deb in front. Pablo was still in astonishment as the group disappeared around the first bend of the trail.

"How in the world did that twelve year old figure it out so fast?" Pablo asked, while handing Clyde the lead rope of the first packhorse out of the trailer.

Clyde, after a long pause, started in. "Did ya see how focused he was? Clearly he was going over and over the sequence of the motion in his head. Having his little brother looking down on him helped. Did ya notice the surprised look on his face for a split second about halfway through? He almost grabbed the horn with his right hand, but at the last moment decided not to and just went for it. Must have seen that part in a video. When everything comes together, it's a great feeling, and he definitely felt it. I call it 'fluid motion.' You'll learn all about that in the kinesiology part of your studies. Also, it's always best to just let things take their course with only minor nudging, especially with the young ones. That allows 'em to save face. They get enough razzing from their siblings and peers, so no need for us adults to pile it on. Now, let's get the pack saddles on these horses, get 'em loaded, and catch up with Deb."

Soon they were on the trail, only about an hour and a half behind the riders. Pablo had gotten used to how rapidly they always caught up with the riders. If the group waited until all the gear was loaded, they would have been that much more behind in the progress of the day. With a larger group, the time difference is much greater. You always have to add to your estimate of the guest riding time. Every stop to pick up a hat and take a pee, all adds up faster than you think. The guides leading the packhorse string never stop for anything. It there is a need to stop, it's only to make a quick adjustment on a pack load.

Sure enough, about an hour and a half later, Pablo and Clyde caught up with Deb and the riders, taking a break at the Woodchuck Creek crossing. The boys were doing good, Dad was pounding his chest with pride, but Mom, however, was starting to suffer. She was grateful to be off the horse, even for a short while. After a fifteen-minute break, and with the saddle cinches reset, the whole group headed up the trail again. Deb continued to lead the riders and stay in front. This section of the trail was dusty, and there was no use making the guests eat the dust of the packhorse string.

Clyde remarked that both boys were riding straight in the saddle and were looking like pros. That was his lead-in for "Let me tell you about the time a guy couldn't stay straight in the saddle to save his life."

Pablo knew there was no escape from another one of Clyde's stories, and knew Deb, up front, was just rolling her eyes and mumbling, "Here we go again."

"The leader of this Sierra Club group," began Clyde, "was getting older and wanted to ride in, but his party members were relatively young. All were to walk in to Red Mountain Basin together with the second in command. Later they would all walk out, but riding in would give the elderly leader a good jump start. Well, this leader touted himself as an experienced horseman, but, all the way in he kept leaning to the right. Since I was behind him, I repeatedly had to ask him to straighten up. This chronic listing to starboard side was not only creating a problem for him and his balance, but it was hell on the horse. The poor horse—I think it was Clipper—kept having her wither pinched by the saddle and had to keep shifting her gait to keep from being forced off balance. I noticed his lifted heel on the right boot, and he confessed he had a short right leg, but since he had this heel lift, all should be even. I advised he wasn't riding on his heel but on the sole of his boot, thus the heel lift was of no help. We stopped and I shortened the right stirrup leather to account for this problem.

"I kept this up for several stops to the point his right leg rode like a jockey. He still leaned to the right. At this time he starts complaining about how it must be the horse's fault, saying she must have a problem with her right shoulder, even though the horse

21

never limped a step. I explained that the horse has been ridden by hundreds of adults, not counting the children she takes out at Dinkey. I was finally able to get him all the way to Red Mountain Basin, but I think I was more worn-out than the horse.

"So, Pablo, that's just what comes with the territory as a packer. Anyway, when I got him unloaded and was starting to head out to find an overnight camp, another hiker came up to me. I recognized him as the one I was to transport out the next day. He pleaded with me that he had reconsidered and wished to go out today instead of tomorrow. The reason was he had a high school reunion scheduled for the next day and was hoping to get to it. I thought to myself, wow, this day just keeps getting better and better. I advised that if we went out this afternoon, it would be well after dark before he got to the trailhead. He understood and was eager to get started. I put him on a different horse than Clipper, figuring she had worked enough today. So, Cowgirl, one of the packhorses that was also an excellent saddle horse, was the choice. She had the lightest load coming in, no more than eighty pounds.

"So, after his one backpack was loaded and he was saddled up, we headed out. After about one hour, Cowgirl was acting like she didn't feel good. I could tell she had all the signs of colic. I immediately stopped and got the rider off the horse. She started to lie down, but I gently got her to keep standing. I wanted to get the saddle off her, which I did in seconds. Down she went again, and I just let her rest there for a few minutes. I retrieved the medicine out of my saddle bag and gave her a heavy dose to relax the intestinal muscles. I also gave her a pain reducer. She started to feel better and stopped her sweating and labored breathing. I knew she wasn't in any shape to get out that day, but also knew she knew the way home. So, I slowly led her a good quarter mile off the trail, to a familiar area. It had grass and a shallow stream, and she had grazed there many times before. She seemed to get the idea and I could tell she started to relax. I removed her halter and gave her a pat on the neck saying, 'Come on home when you feel better.'

"Going back to the string and rider, I put him on my horse. I didn't have the heart to jump on any other horse, cause I knew they had all carried heavy loads all day. After loading Cowgirl's riding saddle on an empty packhorse, I got the lead rope of Mesa, my saddle horse with the anxious rider, and off I started, walking back down the trail with the whole string in tow. This was a six-hour walk out, and it was getting full-on dark with no moon the last two hours.

"When we finally got back to the trailhead, I was definitely tired but still moving. The guest shook my hand vigorously, thanked me for all my trouble, then handed me a check saying give this to Deb and thank her for letting me keep you out so late. I thought that strange but just shrugged my shoulders. It was pitch black and he didn't see anything anyway. After he left, I loaded the horses and got in the cab of the truck. There I could turn on the cab light and read the check. It was a $200 tip and made out to Deborah Clyde. What a piss off. When I got back to the station, I handed her the check and said congratulations.

"Early the next day, I went back up to the trailhead, which is for Clyde Pack Outfit use and is behind a locked gate but with no fence around it. There, standing without a care in the world, was Cowgirl. She had fully recovered and was wondering where I was. I loaded her in the trailer and gave her a much deserved taxi ride back to the station's corral. She got the next week off. Generally colic cases, which are basically spasms in the intestines, are 50 percent fatal. Over the past forty-plus years with my forty-five- to sixty-horse herd, I will get from one to two cases of colic per year. All told, I was not able to help five horses, who passed away from that condition. So, we've been doing real well. I feel the main thing that helps 'em is, after the medicine, to put them in a comfortable environment so they are not bothered with outside stimulus. Being away from humans and even other horses calms them down. When in a corral, I will isolate the horse in an adjacent pen, sometimes with one of their buddies to act as a calming effect. So far, the process has been getting excellent results.

"I tell you all this because not every day is smooth and relaxing. As a packer, you have to take the good with the not so good."

Finally the whole procession came up to a beautiful meadow. It was called MooreBoy Meadow, named after the Moore brothers, who were early cattle ranchers. Pablo remembered this was the same family who were the historic owners of the ranch that Clyde now owned down in the foothills. When they were about two-thirds around the meadow, Clyde motioned for the group to make a left-hand turn off the trail a short distance. There they stopped, dismounted, and tied up the animals for a short break.

Pablo had noticed the same expression on the mother's face that Clyde did. Clyde had many times told him to keep an eye out for the bicycle face, the one you always see on cyclists. Even though they are all suited up fancy with proper riding gear and shiny helmets, for some reason, the same expression is on all the faces. That tortured, I'm in agony look. Clyde has said he admires the willingness of the cyclist to get out and stay in shape, he just never understood why not a single one of 'em looks like they're having fun. A horse ride through the wilderness is supposed to be enjoyable, so Pablo had been conditioned to keep an eye out for any sign of a bicycle face. If you see it, it's time to look for a convenient place to stop and let 'em stretch.

After letting all walk around for a short while, Clyde motioned for the guests to walk over about fifty feet to show them something. Clyde made a general gesture for the group to just look around and tell him if they noticed anything different. The four had blank looks as they gazed about the whole area. Clyde walked three steps and pointed down on the ground. "See this rotten log. Notice if you follow it a new one starts at ninety degrees to it and continues on until another does the same thing. Keep following and a rectangle will become visible. At one end is a pile of rocks. Well, this is what's left of a log cabin and that rock pile is all that is left of the fireplace and chimney. This was the main summer dwelling for the Moore Boys' cattle camp. Over just behind it, you will see remains of a second building. Somewhat smaller but the same basic shape. What's left of a log drift fence can be seen way over at the other side of the meadow. This not only served as a base camp, but a fall holding area as the cattlemen gathered and fed animals here until they had their whole count. Only then did they start the long drive down the mountain to their foothill grazing ranch for the winter.

"A long time ago, a granddaughter of the Moore brothers came to see me as a patient. She showed me a picture of this encampment, and the meadow was packed full of cattle, ready to head down the mountain. Quite a sight. So, during your time up here, pause and take a second and third look at all your surroundings. You might see some carvings on aspen trees put there by the old Basque sheep herders. If you do find one, you have found something that is well over 100 years old. Much like the remains of these cabins. It makes you think about the whole vibrant life that took place up here well before our generation. That's not even considering the signs the Native Americans left here over the 15,000 years they roamed this high country during the summer months."

Just then, almost as if on cue, a woodchuck gave a loud chirp, letting them know his space was being invaded. "Well, Mom," said Clyde, "how're ya doing now? The look on your face tells me you've come back from that dark place you were in."

Mom gave a relieved and grateful smile, signaling she was ready to resume the ride. After checking saddle cinches, and getting all back up on their horses, the group resumed the trek up the trail. As they rode under the looming Loper Peak on the left, Pablo looked back at Clyde, wondering if he would explain the landmark. Clyde only motioned for Pablo to proceed. Pablo explained to the guests about the origin of the name. Being the name of the original white settlers of Coolidge Meadow, which is now under Wishon Lake. He explained that about ninety years ago, the survey crew gave it that name after spending several nights with the family. All this he learned last year from Clyde. After finishing his litany of informative facts, Pablo turned back to see Clyde giving him a thumbs up.

25

Upward they went, zig-zagging with the trail over granite. They finally popped out over a rise and there was Woodchuck Lake, seemingly perched on top of the mountain ridge. What a view to the south and east of the high Sierra peaks. To the west one could look across the San Joaquin Valley and see the California Coast Mountain Range. It was clear today and the group could make out numerous towns across the valley floor.

No one else was around, so the group had the lake to themselves. A suitable campsite was located and the packhorses were soon unloaded. The kids were running down by the lake shore. Dad was standing on a big rock, soaking in the scenery, and Mom was sitting on a log, grateful to be off the horse and starting to feel alive again. Deb walked by her and gave a knowing smile. She told Mom to give it about thirty minutes and she'll feel good as new. Plus, to be grateful she didn't have to walk up here with a loaded backpack. This last statement seemed to do the trick. Mom confessed she never would have made it without the help of Jigger. She then got up, walked over to Jigger, gave him a gentle stroke of his neck, and then planted a kiss right on his cheek. Jigger never flinched, except to move his eyes so as to stare straight into hers. Nothing more needed to be said.

With the horses strung together, the empty saddle horses lined up behind the pack string, Pablo took the lead and started down the trail. He was followed by Clyde, with Deb in the back. She seemed to enjoy this part of the day, being relieved of all the responsibility and only needing to follow along with her riding horse on autopilot.

Pablo noticed Finger Rock way off to his left. He realized he should have mentioned this to the guests, but forgot. It was first named by white men clear back in 1902. Clyde noticed him looking in that direction and somehow could read his mind. Calling out, he said, "That rock has a good backstory, but also serves as a great reference landmark to help keep people from getting lost." Pablo only nodded, knowing he wouldn't miss the opportunity to share that knowledge again.

After about an hour of pleasant, peaceful riding, the silence was broken by Clyde calling out, "Pablo, you know I'm Scottish-American. Did I ever tell ya how the Scots invented the modern world?"

Pablo turned in his saddle to look back, noticing Deb, riding at the end, rolling her eyes and shaking her head as if to say, "Ohhhh, Lord, here we go again."

Clyde, not noticing any of the antics behind him, continued, "Well, you can start with Mr. John Muir himself. Yep, he was born around 1838 in Scotland, and eleven years later his family immigrated to the US. He went on to become the premier naturalist and preservation advocate of modern times. Especially up here in these Sierra Nevada Mountains. He was educated at the University of Wisconsin and thrived on botany and other natural science classes. He didn't jump right into the science world after leaving school, but took jobs doing machine work. Doing this, he got an eye injury that left him blind for a short spell.

"After that he decided to pursue his real love, the natural world. His activism helped create the Yosemite and Sequoia National Parks. He knew how to create friendships with influential people, especially President Theodore Roosevelt. It took multiple years to get things done, but his persistence payed off. As you remember me talking to you last year, he also was a cofounder of the Sierra Club and remained president of the club until he died twenty-two years later. Countless individuals have been inspired by him over the decades. One of them was Ansel Adams. You remember me talking about his son last year up here? Just a few years ago, in April of 2013, the first John Muir Day was celebrated in Scotland.

"Another was Charles Darwin. Remember I talked about him last year? Stood on his grave inside Westminster Abbey in London. Even though he was born in England, he was educated in Scotland. Went to University of Edinburgh for medical school. He tied up with a Scot named Charles Lyell. Sir Lyell was a geologist who impressed Darwin with the concept of gradual geological change. Darwin's theory of natural selection, which conformed

27

with geological change, altered the world's thinking about the origin of our Earth in general. Darwin would go on exploratory trips, something like what folks do here for about one week. Only his lasted five years. Went around the world on a boat named the *HMS Beagle*. Guess the Scots and Brits love dogs too.

"Another Scot," Clyde continued, "Alexander MacKenzie, was a trapper with the Northwest Company, which merged with the Hudson Bay Company. Four out of five of the trappers back then were Scots. Anyway, from the east Canadian coast he went west until he reached Lake Athabasca, which now is in Alberta. He then followed the river out of the lake, which is now called the MacKenzie River, going north to the Arctic Ocean. He then turned west and finally hit the Pacific Ocean. Took him four years. This was while George Washington was being sworn in as our first president. Most of our history books give Lewis and Clark the credit for the first crossing of the North American continent to the Pacific. But the Scot, Alexander MacKenzie, did it ten years earlier.

"Another Scot became the most famous self-made man of all. He was born in Scotland around 1835 and came over here when he was twelve. I'll give you some hints. He initially started working for the railroads. After the Civil War, he sunk his life savings into a new company that made sleeping cars for trains. His business partner was a guy named George Pullman. Within one year this young gentleman had made his first fortune. Looking for somewhere to put his newly earned money, he set his sights on steel. Several fellow Scots joined together, formed a company, and got to work. They knew about English steel manufactories and wanted to be better. In less than twenty years, this one new startup company was producing more steel than half of the production of the entire country of Great Britain. If ya haven't guessed yet, his name was Andrew Carnegie. Founder of US Steel. He kept this up until around 1901, when Mr. Carnegie decided to sell out and retire.

"He did find one person who was able to write him a huge check. His name was J. P. Morgan. After that, Mr. Carnegie showed his true colors. He had a philosophy of 'the man who dies rich dies disgraced.' He put his money where his true legacy turned out to be, in building over 2,600 libraries around the world. Over 2,000 were in the US. Remember, this was when our population was much smaller. He is credited with getting over 35 million people reading books. That's not counting all the parks and auditoriums he built, such as Carnegie Hall in New York. As well as medical research facilities, like the one that made Bellevue Hospital in New York a premier hospital.

"Remember me talking to you about Mount Hutton last year? Ya saw it again the other day. I had mentioned it was named after a geologist, James Hutton, and got the world's attention when he wrote and published his book, *Theory of the Earth*. Well, he was also Scottish born. By the way, his book and teachings also inspired Charles Darwin.

"I could keep going on. There were the Scottish writers. Robert Louis Stevenson, Walter Scott, Robert Burns."

Just then Deb interrupted him by saying, "OK, Allen, let's give it a rest."

Pablo was genuinely interested but didn't protest when Deb intervened. Clyde turned in the saddle to give Deb a questioning look. Deb's response was a quiet one: "No need to keep pushing this Scottish thing on poor Pablo. I think he's heard enough."

Clyde only smiled and replied quietly, "This really has nothing to do with Scottish history."

"Well, what, pray tell, is Pablo to think it has to do with?" Deb whispered in a puzzled response.

Clyde only responded, "Don't worry, he'll figure it out."

Continuing down the trail with the empty pack string then turned into a pleasant, quiet venture. Passing a small grove of aspens, two bucks jumped up from an afternoon slumber. The duo only did three jumps each, then both stopped to stare back at the passing horse string. One had a typical three by three antler rack, high and symmetrical, which was a typical blacktail variety. The other was a different story. He was at least a head taller than his buddy, with a thick neck and huge shoulders. His antlers went straight sideways from the base, where at least three-inch eye guards were plainly visible. They didn't curve up until at least a foot out from both sides, at which point they forked and then forked again. This made a perfect four by four rack, the likes of which one seldom sees. His ears were much larger and he had a Roman-type nose.

After a prolonged silence, with all standing still and looking at each other, Clyde spoke up. "There, Pablo, is a perfect example of a western blacktail deer and a mule deer, side by side. When they are visible like this the difference is dramatic. The blacktail is native to this part of the US. Some think the mule deer originally migrated over here from the Rockies, which is probably true. Hunters will come up here, stomp around these mountains for generations, and never see a darn thing. The issue is they don't get very far from their cars. Those are the same people who think all the deer are gone from the Sierras, but right there is proof they're full of crap. Just nowadays they are harder to see from the road."

Pablo only got started after a long pause. He didn't want the moment to end, but the deer made the decision first. They slowly walked off back into the grove like they didn't have a care in the world. Down the trail they all went, all feeling the relaxed state of mind when a packer doesn't have the responsibility of people and their gear to worry about. After crossing Woodchuck Creek and ultimately leaving the wilderness and entering the front country, the spike station soon came into view. Unsaddling and loading all went smoothly. Coming into the station, the trio was greeted by the two excited dogs. Deb was dropped off at the cookhouse door to start dinner, which she had pre-prepared. Pablo and Clyde unloaded and unsaddled the stock. After feeding the horses, only then was the day's work over, as the sun was setting. After a hardy dinner, Pablo again gave a wide-mouth yawn, declaring how tired he was. Clyde and Deb only looked at each other, both knowing this was only an excuse.

The sun had set, leaving total darkness. Looking across the compound, Clyde noticed a small reading light still on at Pablo's desk. There, through the small window, Clyde could see Pablo staring at his computer screen. Inside Pablo had anxiously typed in the Google search for anything and everything to reveal the subject matter so dominant in his mind: Mexican-American contributions to the modern world.

Shoeing a horse

JEFFREY PINE

Claudia Fletcher

CHAPTER 3

Leave-It-Right

Pablo was amazed when he first popped open his eyes after a deep sleep. It was 4:59 a.m. He had never gotten used to the wonderment of the internal clock. Or, maybe it was Clyde walking past the window on his way to the corral. Whatever. Time to rise and shine.

Clyde greeted him with a handful of lead ropes as he walked up. "There's eight guys out in the tent cabins, all still asleep. They howled until late last night, so must be sleeping off a hangover. Don't worry, we'll get 'em going on time. Kicking 'em up early with their heads throbbing never gets old," Clyde commented with a slight grin. "Generally a nice group of folks on the whole, but a couple of the leaders are sure full of themselves. When they arrived last night, those two didn't waste any time informing me of how experienced they were. Their gear is all top-shelf and brand-new. One of the leaders was bragging how much he paid for some of the items. I'm sure the sporting goods store looked out the front window and saw him coming. Anyway, I told 'em to have all their gear on the loading dock here by 7:00 a.m. It's gonna be fun pushing 'em to be on time. Found out what they all do down in Los Angeles. Seems they're all camera crew for TV and movie set companies. According to them, the whole industry would fall apart without their personal involvement. Just ask 'em.

"We're taking them to Rock Lake over in the Dinkey Lakes Wilderness, as per their request. All of 'em are walking, so we're just hauling gear and that means Deb gets the day off. Not having to babysit these arrogant guys didn't seem to hurt her feelings much.

"I figure five packhorses should do it. Let's pull out Diamond X, Loper, Pearl, Sundown, and Tobacco. Mesa is good to go for you. I'll take Harley."

While the duo was putting on the pack saddles, Clyde mentioned, "Last night these guys asked about the fishing. That's all they cared about. After that discussion I let 'em know that being early in the season, and right after a heavy, late snow pack, the mosquitos were going to be out with a vengeance. The main leader just shrugged his shoulders and replied it would be no problem, reminding me again how experienced they were. I just smiled and dropped the subject."

By 6:45, all seven horses were saddled and loaded into the gooseneck trailer. Clyde looked out across the station to the tent cabins and shook his head.

"Well, Pablo, time to go get the darlings up. Doesn't look like they'll make it on their own."

As Clyde walked up to the tents, purposefully stomping his feet, he yelled out, "Time to rise and shine, ladies. Horses told me they are leaving in fifteen minutes and trust me, they mean it."

Both tents jumped alive as if someone poked two beehives with a stick. By 7:00, all the gear was piled on the loading dock. Most of the guys stumbled as they walked and Pablo wondered how they would ever make the hike up to the lake. While getting the paperwork done, which always included a section on wilderness rules and etiquette, Pablo noticed the leaders' body language of not being interested and annoyed for the short delay. Finally, the group staggered to their cars and drove to the trailhead to start the hike. With relief, all was quiet again at the station.

With the calm, packing the gear went smoothly for Clyde and Pablo. After loading it on the flatbed, they were ready to roll out by 7:30. Stopping by the cookhouse on the way out, Pablo got the lunches while Clyde gave Deb a kiss and grabbed the two-way radios. Dinkey eagerly jumped into the back of the truck and off they went.

While on the eight-mile haul, Pablo spoke up first. "These young guys look like they're in terrible shape for the hike after a long night of partying. Why would they even consider being so foolish in this altitude? I can almost feel their heads pulsating from here. I'm a good ten years younger than they are and even I have more sense than that."

Clyde pondered for a short while, then replied. "I guess with some young folks, they have more energy than good sense. But remember, the older ya get, you may have more sense but less energy. I figure it's just the ying and yang of life. Look at those deer coming down from high on the mountain there to the left. They look chipper this bright sunny morning. Doubt if they were partying last night."

As they pulled into the spike station at the trailhead, Pablo noticed the clients' cars were parked and they had already started hiking. He gave a short sigh of relief, glad the group had made it that far.

Loading up the gear onto the packhorses went smoothly. Pablo was impressed with the high-end quality of their gear. Included were four large, thick-walled ice chests that were padlocked, which was supposed to make 'em bear proof. That's what the leader claimed the salesman guaranteed. We'll see, Pablo thought.

After about one hour up the trail, on the backside of Courtright Lake, the riders came upon two bridges. These were put in by the Forest Service to keep travelers up above the soft meadow zone the trail spanned. They were constructed entirely with natural logs from the immediate area. Good idea but a terrible design. The underlying stringer logs were good but the whole top surface was made of up of smaller, round logs set sideways down the whole length. It looked real nice but was torture to walk on for man and beast. Perfectly set up to roll an ankle. Pablo noticed the rutted side routes on the left and right of each bridge where people chose to reroute. Obviously the bridges didn't solve the problem; in fact, they made it worse. Now there were two trails through this sensitive area instead of one.

Clyde noticed Pablo's focus on the situation and spoke up. "The Forest Service says it's too expensive to come in here and fix this. Look off to your left. You'll see the remains of the bridges before these two. They were built in the exact same way. Some higher-ups never seem to learn. They're the ones who make the decisions for the wilderness, but they're also the ones who spend the least amount of time up here. I call it 'backwards line of command,' and it mostly never works. I've been giving my opinion of how to fix this repeatedly over the last five years, but the high-ups just keep waving me off.

"So Pablo, how would you solve this problem?"

Pablo slowed his lead horse to a crawl, then completely stopped, with the whole string on the bridge, perfectly still. Clyde was on the last animal, standing in the middle of the second bridge. Finally, Pablo nudged Mesa and moved the string off the bridge until Harley was off the end, then came to a complete stop again. He turned in the saddle to look back and said, "Well, the basic underlying structure of the bridge is in good shape. Some of the top cross-logs are broken, but that's not a big problem. I'd use two-inch by twelve-inch planks, about twelve-footers, and line 'em up side by side down the middle the whole length of each bridge. Need to measure, but I'd guess about ten of 'em would be enough. See how the nails here lift up due to the expansion and contraction of the winter snows? Would be best to screw 'em all in good and tight. Forget the spike nails. All they end up being is toe stubbers. With the flat planks down the center, three feet wide, it's plenty of room to walk on by humans and horses."

Looking back, Pablo could only notice Clyde's expressionless face. That's when Clyde asked, "Well, Pablo, how would you get the planks here?"

Pablo thought for a moment, then a light went on in his mind. "The lake is right there. Could bring 'em over by boat. There's plenty of fourteen-foot fishing boats around. Those planks would fit in 'em easy." Pablo, being quite proud of himself, looked back, only to be greeted with the same stare.

Clyde spoke up again. "OK, but what about the Forest Services aversion about having milled wood in the wilderness?"

Pablo was initially deflated, but suddenly snapped out of it. "Wait a minute, the wilderness boundary is still about a quarter mile up the trail. This is front country and thus not a problem." Pablo was really puffed up now but, after looking back, was still only rewarded with Clyde's continued blank stare.

"What about the Forest Service's go-to excuse of not having any manpower due to funding shortages?" asked Clyde.

Pablo was stopped cold by this reality, which always came up. But then, with a renewed eagerness in his voice, he replied, "I remember last year you said volunteer groups were always looking for a project in the forest. A handful of six to eight people, after a small fundraiser to gather a few hundreds dollars for the lumber, could knock this project out in one day and have plenty of time left over for their beer."

Pablo again looked back, but this time was met with a big grin from Clyde. "Bingo," Clyde said. "That's exactly the pitch I've been giving for the past five years. Things are finally coming around though. This whole project should happen shortly. Stuff takes forever to get done with the government. There's one more piece to the puzzle needed and with that I'm finally getting there. Ya have to let 'em think it was all their idea from the start. Every one of our presidents recognized that fact. Ronald Reagan said, 'If you want something good to get done, let someone else have the credit.' That way they have a personal ownership and will make sure it's done right. Always a good go-to if you're stuck.

"Don't pay any mind to my continued questioning. It's just a way of leading you through the thought process. Some call it grilling. You'll get plenty of that in med school and residency, trust me. But don't worry, you'll do just fine."

Within an hour the pack string came upon the hikers. Two were lying in the shade, looking like pure crap. The leader of the group said he thought the two had either altitude sickness or drank some bad water. Clyde responded, "Ya, they most likely drank some bad water—last night. Hey you two, I doubt you're gonna die, you'll only wish you would. Just take it easy and stay together. You're over halfway there. We'll see ya on the way back." Then Clyde motioned to Pablo to start moving again.

After about four turns in the trail, Pablo turned in the saddle and asked, "Do you think those two are sick?"

Clyde answered, "Sure they are, but it has nothing to do with the altitude or bad water. It's called a hangover. Some people come up here and think there's no added price to pay for foolish behavior. Put some added physical exertion together with this altitude and soon you will reevaluate dumb decisions. Those two didn't have any GI, respiratory, or cerebral issues. But, if they haven't improved by the time we get back, we'll take 'em out with us. I seriously doubt that will be necessary."

Going past Cliff Lake, the string began the climb up and over the ridge and down to their destination, Rock Lake. Pablo always loved seeing the hemlock trees only found in this area at Rock Lake. This, added to the quartz crystals found naturally here, made this place extra special. The lake was seated perfectly at the bottom of a geographic bowl, with only a small opening for the exit stream. One of the most picturesque lakes he had ever seen.

They unloaded the gear at a campsite on the far side, well away from the lake and with nice protection from the wind and sun. It was also upslope enough to lessen the mosquito problem. With the tarps folded, the ropes rolled up, and all stuffed into the empty pack bags, the string was turned around and headed back. They soon encountered the group at the top of the ridge. The two hikers looked better and were most likely going to make it. Clyde reconfirmed the pickup date in a week and off the two groups went in opposite directions.

The three-hour ride out went smoothly. Going over the two bridges, Pablo glanced back at Clyde, who gave him a smile with a thumbs up. Dinkey trotted along behind Clyde, wagging her tail, just happy to be there. At the spike station, unloading the gear and putting the horses in the trailer went easy as usual. The animals always seemed to know when the day was about over and were eager to get back to the corral with their feed bins loaded with the best alfalfa hay money could buy. Pablo felt he could load the whole string in the trailer by just pointing 'em in the right direction and turning them loose, and they would all jump in by themselves. He had seen Clyde do this a few times with his saddle horse, but had just thought it was a fluke. Someday he might try it, but only if he was alone. That way there would not be any witnesses if things got screwed up.

The drive down the eight-mile run to the station was always relaxing. Clyde just set the switch for the exhaust brake on the truck and kept his foot off the gas peddle. He could control the speed with only the on/off switch. All the way down the eight miles he never touched the brake peddle. This made for an easy, smooth ride for both him and Pablo and the horses. Dinkey always loved this part, with her nose out the side and ears flapping. Pablo never understood why this felt good to the dog. But, don't knock it if you haven't tried it. Maybe someday he would. Of course, there couldn't be any witnesses.

Back at the station, with the horses unsaddled, turned out in the corral, and munching contently, all was good for the day. After dinner, Pablo went to bed and was fast asleep before the count of five.

Two afternoons later, suddenly the group of eight guys from Rock Lake came into the station headquarters. The leaders were full of complaints about how the mosquitos were eating them alive and none of 'em could take it any longer. The fishing was great but the mosquitos were too much. They also declared they would need two fewer packhorses for the way back since they had eaten all the food and that left room in the chests to pack other gear. Clyde questioned them on how they could have eaten a week's worth of food in two days. They all looked at each other and the leader said they just forced it down. Clyde gave a skeptical look and said, "We'll see." Clyde said he could go in the next day and for them to go hang out in the tent cabins until his return tomorrow afternoon.

Back up the trail the duo went the next day. Clyde had taken all five packhorses, for he privately told Pablo he didn't believe their story about the food. Pablo had wondered why both dogs, Dinkey and Pasty, were brought along. Clyde had told him they had a purpose.

Arriving at the Rock Lake camp around noon, Pablo began unloading the empty gear from the packhorses. He noticed Clyde motioning for the dogs to head outside the camp area for some reason. It didn't take long for Clyde to notice a lot of commotion by the dogs behind a huge boulder about twenty yards above camp. Pablo noticed Clyde walking up to the area. Soon Clyde was motioning for Pablo to come up, he had something for him to see.

Walking up, Pablo was shocked at the sight. There, piled high, was all the raw food dumped out from the ice chests. Most of the wrappers had been removed, but it was still starting to smell. What made that worse was all around the area was toilet paper and human waste. No effort was made to bury anything. Ya, they used this area as a bathroom, then lastly dumped all their unused food. Clyde motioned for Pablo to take a look at the bigger picture, declaring, "Notice the slope of the land. After a heavy rain over what's left of the snow pack, all this refuse has only one place to wash. Right into the lake. I call this an outright criminal assault on the wilderness. But, I have a better form of punishment. We're getting the shovel they have in the gear pile but chose to not use, and bringing it up here with all four of the empty ice chests."

The duo went to work shoveling up all the rotting food and filling each of the four chests to about three-fourths full. Then came the best part. They gently shoveled all the poop piles with toilet

40

paper into the remaining room of each of the chests. With this unpleasant job done, Clyde shut the lids on the chests. That's when Pablo actually noticed the YETI brand name on each of the chests.

Clyde secured the padlocks, and then said with a grin, "Let's get these chests and the other gear loaded and get gone." While Pablo was handing Clyde some bags for loading, one of the zippers was wide open and when he lifted it, a whole pile of rocks fell out onto the ground. Clyde came over to look at what came out and Pablo could almost see steam coming out of his ears. Clyde responded, "Now I'm really pissed. Look at those rocks. Every one of 'em is almost gem quality quartz crystal. Removing these from the wilderness is a federal offense. That's why they are called leave-it-rights. That means, leave 'em right where you found them. Pablo, gather all of them up and take them back up to the cliff edge and scatter 'em where they came from."

By the time Pablo got back, Clyde had finished loading and tying the string. He hopped on his saddle horse and Clyde handed him the lead rope to the sting before getting on his own mount. Off they went back down the trail.

Pulling into the station was going to be interesting. The group all walked up to meet the rig with their gear. After unloading it all back onto the loading dock, Clyde waited until he had all of their attention.

"Young men," Clyde began, "I want each of you to learn something today. Those ice chests are locked for a reason. I wouldn't open any of them if I were you. They are full of what all you left back at the lake. Including your poop. I suggest you take every one of those expensive chest and deposit them in the nearest dumpster on your way home. As for those quartz crystals you pilfered from the wilderness, I took the liberty of redepositing them back to their original location. What you did is not only against the wilderness law, it's disrespectful to the forest and the general public who uses it. If any of you object and want to complain to the Forest Service, be my guest. In fact, I'd be glad to call the Forest Service Law

Enforcement Officer over here and you can talk to him directly. If that is your choice, you'd better be talking fast, while he's writing up your fat ticket or, worse, putting you all in handcuffs for your taxi ride down to the county jail. There you're welcome to plead your case in front of the federal magistrate judge. One last thing. I don't *ever* want to see any of you back up here again. If I do, I promise I won't be so pleasant. Now get this crap picked up and get the hell out of here before I really go ballistic."

Pablo had subconsciously looked at his watch and noticed it took exactly six minutes for the group to load all the stuff and be out the gate of the station.

That done, Clyde turned to Pablo and replied, "That's a lesson those eight will never forget. Hopefully, whenever any of them reproduce, they will relay this learning experience so their children will respect the woods and the public who use it. If they don't, then God help the wilderness. That group feels they control the entertainment world because they man the cameras. Well, ya never know, maybe some day I'll produce a TV film—about them. Anyway, let's get these horses unloaded, unsaddled, and out to feed. Lord knows, they have deserved it after hauling other peoples crap all day—literally."

The next day was bright and beautiful. No trips were scheduled, so Pablo had the day off. Sitting at the kitchen table after breakfast, holding his last cup of coffee, Pablo wondered what to do with his day. Deb noticed the perplexed look on his face and spoke up. "Want a suggestion for today?" Pablo nodded his head and shrugged his shoulders. Deb continued while Clyde sat across from him, not saying a word. "How about taking a fishing pole, a chair, and one of your textbooks for next semester's classes, go find a shady spot by the lake, and read and fish?"

Pablo thought about this for a moment, then replied, "That sounds like fun, but I don't have any idea where a good fishing spot might be. Everywhere I know, I'd have to ride a horse too."

Deb answered, "You might want to go down by the boat

launching ramp. I've heard the fishing has been good there." Pablo didn't take long to ponder that idea before getting up and saying, "I think I'll do just that," and left the room after depositing his empty coffee cup in the sink.

Clyde, still motionless, looked up at Deb after the door closed behind Pablo and said, "You know the fishing is not that great there. With all the commotion along the boat ramp, he's not going to catch anything."

Deb just smiled. "Most likely not, but he will get a great show watching all the people try to launch boats down that narrow one-lane ramp."

After parking his truck by the lake, Pablo walked up to the ramp area and noticed a perfect lodgepole pine tree with shade and a level area at the base for his lawn chair. There, with a ringside view of the ramp, he sat down and cast out his line, letting the weighted bait settle to the point where the bobber float was all that remained on the surface. He opened his physics textbook to chapter one. This was going to be a tough subject to get through, so he might as well get started early, he thought. A gentle breeze came up, which felt good, reminding him it was probably going to be a warmer-than-usual day.

After thirty minutes of being totally absorbed in his textbook,

LODGEPOLE PINE

43

and only giving occasional glances to his motionless bobber, Pablo was interrupted by the first of the boats on trailers being lined up to back down the ramp. Not giving it much thought, he went back to his reading. Soon he was interrupted again by a commotion on the ramp. The husband was on his third attempt of backing down his trailer, trying to launch his fourteen-foot aluminum fishing boat. This little boat was being towed by a brand-new, three-quarter-ton pickup. The truck was tricked out to the hilt, boasting pin stripes and jacked up with huge balloon tires. Pablo wondered if the driver's ears popped whenever he climbed up and into the cab. Surely there must be a ladder that came out from underneath.

The guy was cussing up a storm, clearly heard through the open window. Seems each time he tried, the more jackknifed the rig ended up. Pablo could see he was way overcorrecting on the steering, which made it worse every time. He had learned how to do this maneuver from hard experience backing up the stock trailers. Pablo could hear the man direct his wife to get out and guide him better. Somehow, it seemed, the whole fiasco was her fault. She got out and went to the back, standing so as to be visible in his side-view mirror. The fourth attempt didn't show much improvement, even though she was waving frantically to turn the opposite direction. The left wheel of the trailer was soon completely off the ramp and hanging over the edge of the two-foot drop-off, resting on the axle. Meanwhile, two more cars with boats were waiting at the top of the ramp, their occupants clearly getting frustrated with the delay.

The husband jumped out of the cab, slammed the door shut, gave his poor wife a disrespectful hand gesture, and stomped off into the trees to sit down. All of which further exasperated the fishermen waiting above. His wife, with hands on hips, tapped her right foot for a few seconds, then made her move. She walked up to the cab and got in, started the engine, and moved forward, scraping the trailer axle a little but causing no damage. The wheel soon popped back up onto the ramp. She moved the whole outfit up to straighten everything out, and then slowly started her descent down the ramp, with only minor corrections with the steering wheel. Gradually the boat slipped into the water and started to float off the trailer. She then got out, unhooked the bow line from the trailer winch, and snapped a small rope to the bow metal loop. She then walked sideways over to the floating dock next to the ramp and tied off. She returned to the truck, climbed in, and pulled the empty trailer back up and into the parking lot. She was met with cheers from awaiting fisherman as she drove by.

When she came walking back, not even looking at her still-sitting husband, she proceeded to the boat, climbed in, started the motor, and slowly backed away from the dock. That got her husband up off his rear end and jogging down to the dock. She then slowly returned to the dock, allowing him to climb aboard. All noticed how he took a seat in the front while she continued to pilot from the rear, right hand on the motor handle. Turning the craft around smoothly, she began the slow chug out across the lake. Not one of the anxious fisherman on top of the ramp moved. All just stood, staring at the small boat getting smaller, going out across the water. The husband never moved, sitting still with his head down. The wife had her head on a swivel, obviously enjoying the quiet scenery as it floated by from her captain's perch.

The boat was a tiny speck before the next fisherman came out of his trance and began backing his boat down the ramp. His progress was extremely slow. Pablo figured he didn't want to make the mistakes of his predecessor in front of the same audience. All went well for him.

The third boat came down in a direct line and much faster. Seemed the driver felt he had all under control, judging by the way his chin was up and his shoulders were out, and how he took only an occasional glance at either side-view mirror. Down the boat went into the water. The farther he backed up the deeper in the water the boat went, not giving any indication it was going to float at all. Down, down it went. Finally the guy from the previous launch, still on the floating dock, was waving frantically at the driver, yelling that his boat was filling with water and he better pull back out while he still could. The driver shifted from reverse to drive and began pulling forward, barely making progress with the heavily laden boat, which by now was almost half full of water. Finally the rear of the boat cleared the water line and out the back came two high powered streams of water. Seems he forgot to replace the drain plugs after his last use. He was encouraged to just pull out to the parking lot by the now four-deep awaiting fisherman at the top of the ramp.

The next three launches went smoothly, except for one guy who thought it was a good idea to load the boat with the camping equipment from the back of the pickup *after* the boat was launched. Pablo figured this was a big no-no, judging from the bombardment of cursing from the fisherman waiting above.

By now Pablo had lost all interest in his physics book, and never even gave a glance toward his fishing bobber.

Down came another launch attempt. This one came so fast, Pablo was wondering if he was going to stop at all and just launch his car into the lake too. Into the water the boat went, where it started to float. All was well, except that under the boat was the still-attached trailer! Seems he forgot to unfasten the tie-down straps. Pulling back up and stopping, the driver went to the rear of the trailer and unfastened the straps, then did a redo on the launch.

By this time it was late afternoon and the boat launches tapered off to almost nil. Pablo's fishing bobber was still frozen in the same spot where it had landed several hours before. With only three pages read in his text, he decided it was pointless to continue. Having had enough excitement for one day, he stood up, stretched, reeled in his line, folded up his chair, and began the short walk to the truck. He felt he had just been to the circus, and the best part was it was free.

Deb met him with a grin as he walked into the pack station cookhouse. "Well," she said, "I don't see any fish."

Pablo pondered a moment, then replied, "No, didn't catch any fish, but I did catch an eye full of human behavior."

Deb continued her uninterrupted smile. Pablo then felt as if she had been there all along and didn't need any elaboration of the day's events. He just returned the smile, shook his head, and sauntered out the back door.

Trail duck markers

"DINKEY"

Claudia Fletcher
2019

"PATSY"

Claudia Fletcher

CHAPTER 4

Middle Fork of the Kings River

Pablo took pride in being out at the corral by 4:55 a.m., ready to get started. Clyde handed him two lead ropes and started in on answering the question he knew he would ask. "We're going to be out five days this trip. Taking two guys from LA who requested a special adventure. It'll be one for us as well. You've never seen this country we're heading into. Except for the beginning and the end, all of it will be in the Kings Canyon National Park. Ya've been to Tehipite Valley. Well, we are going there for the first night. Then, day two, up to a place called Simpson Meadow. Then the third day we'll take 'em up to the Palisades Creek area. It's up where the Middle Fork of the Kings Rivers crosses the John Muir Trail. Some call that part the Pacific Crest Trail. We'll drop off the clients there. That last part will take us half a day. Then we retrace our steps, empty, back down to Simpson, and the last night we'll be coming out from Tehipite Valley.

"These adventurous guys are going to start backpacking from up on the PCT. Plan to meet up with them ten days later over in Red Mountain Basin. They're going on over through Evolution Valley, then up the trail to Mount Goddard and out over Hell for Sure Pass to meet up with us again in Red Mountain Basin. Quite a trip for them and also for you, cause you'll see country that will make your eyes pop out. Only need one packhorse for their gear, since it's just two backpacks. We'll need one packhorse for our gear and four saddle horses. Only taking the A team this trip. You remember the Tehipite cliff trail from last year? Well, the rest of it is just as scary. Get Pearl and Diamond X for the two packhorses. You'll ride Jay and I'll take Jigger. The clients can use Trapper and Howdy. So, let's get started."

Saddling up all six horses went fast. The clients were ready and eager to get started. With Pablo getting the food sack for the five days, and Clyde giving Deb a goodbye kiss, out the gate they went by 7:15 a.m., the clients following. No dogs this trip, since they were not allowed in the national park. Dinkey and Patsy sat on the porch looking dejected. Deb was giving 'em a comforting pat on their heads as the group headed out.

Getting things loaded at the Rancheria Trailhead only took twenty minutes since it was just their gear and the clients' two back-packs. Before 8:30 they were heading up the trail, Pablo in the lead. Cinches were reset just before crossing Rancheria Creek, about one hour up the trail. With an easy trail on a beautiful day, the ride was quite pleasant. The clients had been with Clyde before, so much time was spent catching up on life since their last trip. Mainly the

talk was about the businesses they were in and what their kids had been up to.

The route took them by Cow Meadow and Wet Meadow on the way to Crown Valley. Pablo often spotted pine marten as they made their way through this area. Arriving at Crown Valley was always interesting. Clyde would stop here to give the horses a break, and let the clients overview the log

50

cabins belonging to the Johnson family. This was a private property wilderness inholding, there before the Wilderness Act. The trail through the property is a public easement. Clyde, respecting the property rights of the owners, never took clients over to the cabins, so all stayed on the trail.

Continuing on, the group crossed Rodgers Creek, named after an old sheepman. Pablo remembered another Johnson land inholding, which they would not see today since it was on the other way to Blue Canyon. This other inholding was much smaller, about forty acres, and had one log cabin. Been called Scotty's cabin all this time. Scotty never owned the land, just had somewhat of an agreement with the Johnsons to put a cabin there. He must have passed away a long time ago, since Clyde said he never met him and never saw people staying here.

Soon they came to the Kings Canyon National Park boundary sign. Basically, from this point on the wilderness was controlled by the National Park Service (which is a part of the Department of the Interior, not the US Forest Service). The wind coming up the canyon gave Pablo the first hint they were getting close to the rim of Tehipite, and reminded him of the powerful forces that lay ahead.

Clyde stopped in a somewhat flat area just before the rim and had the two clients dismount. "From here on to the bottom, you both have to walk," Clyde declared. "Far too dangerous to ride down this cliff trail, especially for you guys who only ride once every few years. Soon as you get started, you'll see why and thank me for getting ya off your horse." Sensing the ominous tone of Clyde's voice, there was no argument from the clients. Pablo, remembering this section from last year, noticed his mouth suddenly getting dry, making it hard to swallow. By this time he could hear the roar of the Kings River below, which made the ever-increasing wind in the trees seem like a minor sound in comparison. Clyde carefully led his saddle horse to the front of the line and instructed Pablo to take up the rear. The two packhorses were to stay in the front behind Clyde, to be followed by the empty saddle horses. The saddle stirrups were tied over the saddles to prevent hangups, and the bridles were removed and tied on to the saddle horns. This allowed free movement of the horse's head, which it needed for balance. The lead ropes were also coiled and tied to the saddles. These horses were veterans and knew to simply follow the horse in front. Clyde instructed the clients it would be safer to follow behind the horses. He didn't want them in front and downtrail, fearing the horses would kick rocks loose which could potentially become fatal missiles. Clyde looked back at Pablo, waved the "Let's go" arm motion, and disappeared over the edge. That's when a large lump jumped up Pablo's throat, which he swallowed down. He lowered his chin and nudged Jay forward. As Pablo went over the rim, he knew the clients were right behind him. All he heard was one gasping to the other, saying, "Holy crap."

Down the narrow switchbacks they went. It never ceased to amaze Pablo how the horses could maintain such good footing and not stumble on the narrow trail, which was only six inches wide in places and often strewn with loose rock. Knowing his life was in Jay's care, he could only trust and keep leaning back in the saddle, feet forward and the reins loose, allowing Jay to keep his balance. The last thing you want to do is start jerking around the reins. It only gets the horse upset and forces his attention to go to you and not the trail. That's when riding animals lose focus, slip, and go over the edge, carrying you with 'em. It was easy to understand why Clyde never let clients ride up or down this section. With their inexperience, a serious problem was almost an eventual certainty.

Soon, a nice little flat came into view. Pablo remembered it from last year. It was the only place to safely stop and check the loads and cinches. To view your starting point, one only had to look almost straight up. The two hikers soon caught up with them and all sat down for a short rest. One of them pulled out his water bottle and took a long drink. Clyde gently advised him to slow down on that, since it was only going to get much rougher and hotter as they continued down. Don't overhydrate, which is a common mistake. The hiker gave a surprised look, blinked, then nodded understandingly and replaced the cap on the bottle. "Also," Clyde explained, "there's not one drop of water on this trail until you get to the river ya see down between your feet."

That convinced him and the subject never needed to be brought up again. With the horses rested, Clyde and Pablo remounted and continued down the trail. Pablo could see again the yucca plants he remembered from last year. This area had all been burnt over several years ago but was recovering well. With the unforgiving nature of the no-room-for-error trail they were on, Pablo was grateful Clyde had double checked with the Park Service about their clearing this trail three weeks earlier. To have a major obstacle here could be catastrophic. He understood why the Park Service trail crew had their own name for this section. They called it the "Son-of-a-Bitch." Quite fitting, Pablo thought.

Down the group went, kicking rocks off the edges as they went in their semi-controlled fall. The farther down they went, the more loose shale was on the trail. The horses were almost sliding on their butts through several sections. On a switchback during all this commotion, Clyde looked back up at a wide-eyed Pablo, and with a grin remarked, "Glad we don't have to haul heavy loads back up this lovely route. That would make this trip we're doing right now seem like a mere stroll in the park. Going up loaded, the poor horses would have to lunge and jump the whole way, gaining two steps and sliding back one each time. That's why, when we come back out, it'll be early in the morning, maybe even still somewhat dark. All to take advantage of the coolest time of the day. If we tried it in the afternoon, it'd be so hot, like Robin Williams said in *Good Morning, Vietnam*, 'You could bake bread in our underwear.'"

Finally hitting bottom, Clyde pulled the string to a stop, hopped off, and tied the lead ropes of the two loose saddle horses to a dead but sturdy tree. There they waited until the hikers caught up, which took over an hour. Glad to be near the finish line, the hikers remounted and continued the remaining forty-five-minute ride to the camp. This was the same spot Pablo was at last year, with the loud river nearby and an unobstructed view of Tehipite Dome over-head. With a heavy breeze to keep the bugs away, a good night's sleep was in store. As he lay in his insect-protective tent, Pablo felt lucky to have survived another trip down to this hole. He slept soundly, never hearing if the horses were eating acorns or caring if any bear came by.

The early morning sun was just lighting up the top of Tehipite Dome, giving it the appearance of a radiant cap. Clyde was already up and had the horses unhobbled, tied up, and ready to be saddled. The clients were just staggering out of their tents, stretching and heading toward the river for water. Clyde motioned for Pablo to get up and get his coffee cup so he could fill it. The clients sat around the morning fire, questioning Clyde on the day's travel. He told 'em today's ride to Simpson wouldn't be so bad. The trail follows the river all the way up. It's quite narrow but not bad. Main thing is getting going early, for it gets hot down in this canyon during the midday. They would like to get to Simpson Meadow before midafternoon.

With that, the group commenced to load up. With Clyde in the lead, Pablo was in the back, to keep a close eye on the riders just in front of him. The first major creek crossing was Silver Spring Falls. This is the dumping point for Crown Creek into the Kings River. Crown Creek originates from the Forest Service side. The water was about two and a half feet deep and filled with large, slick, moss-covered rocks on the bed. The horses slipped a little. That was of no concern to Clyde, but the clients were white-knuckled. About fifty yards down the trail, after exiting the creek, the clients started to relax and began jabbering.

Clyde started to explain, over the loud river roar, about the Indian painted rocks not too far from this location, over near the river. It had taken him several different outings to finally find them. Somewhat of a dis-appointment though. They just looked like

COFFEE POT

three oak leaves about the size of your fist, lined up side by side. He was amazed that it was the only evidence of native American art he could find here, especially with all the hundreds of years they spent in the area. Clyde explained that it was his guess that they didn't feel the need to mark up their surroundings like we seem to do.

Soon they passed Blue Canyon Falls. This creek came from Blue Canyon, originating up on the north side of the park, and also emptied into the Kings River. The route seemed to get a reasonable amount of travel, but was maintained only once every three years. When you have a narrow gorge with cliffs on one side and a raging river on the other, getting a large tree crossways in the trail can be a serious problem. Fortunately, the trail crew had been through earlier this season and things were relatively clean. It's about twelve and a half miles to Simpson Meadow, and takes all day since the going is slow beside this raging river, so loud that one has to shout to be heard from only a few feet away.

Pablo remembered Deb talking about taking mapmaker Tom Harrison into the Dinkey Lakes area a few years earlier. He would measure all the routes and put mileages on his trail maps. Some folks think this is all they need to time out their trips, but mileage is only one factor. The difficulty of the route is the biggest contributor to how far one can get from point A to point B. Deb would say, "Average hiking time would be more valuable information." But Mr. Harrison only would respond with, "Average hikers think they can translate the distance with hiking in the flatlands to the same up in rough high country. They never seem to accept it, so I simply put in measured distances." Pablo understood why Clyde would always say how hard it is to convince folks to not overestimate their travel goals for each day, but most won't listen. That is especially true in this canyon, for not only do you have to worry about the loose rocks and cliffs plunging into the river, but rattlesnakes too. One always has to pay attention where you place each step, and this takes time. But on the plus side, stopping often to gaze up the canyon walls has it rewards and adds to the wonder of the trip.

By about four in the afternoon they finally come into Simpson Meadow. With the horses unsaddled and hobbled out for the evening and camp set up, the group was finally able to settle down for the evening after a long, hot, and hard day. The air was cooler since they had gained some altitude after leaving Tehipite Valley. Sitting around a small campfire, Clyde explained some history of the original owner of this valley.

"John Greenup Simpson came to California in 1850, obviously looking for gold. He soon found something much better, fantastic grazing land for cattle. He went back to his home state of Kentucky, organized a wagon train, and started back in 1852. Along the way they were attacked by Indians somewhere in the Southwest. Their cattle and horses were driven off but no one was killed. They had no choice but to start walking. One of the group was a two-year-old child who became ill and died. She was buried somewhere in Arizona. The group was found by soldiers and taken to an Army post. There Simpson was able to obtain horses and provisions and continued his trip.

"He finally made it to his destination at the base of the Sierra Nevada mountains in Fresno County. Since he was here early, there was a lot of land available and at a good price. Mr. Simpson was able to purchase 7,000 acres, build a home, and start his cattle business. In a few years, he went to the neighboring town of Visalia, where he found his future bride, Sarah. They had three children. John would later be elected Fresno County Supervisor. After all this he passed away in 1877 when he was only forty-seven years old. The following generations of Simpsons kept the ranch going until 1950, when all was sold out. Their high country headquarters for the cattle operation was down at Dinkey Creek. How they got cattle clear up to this meadow I have not been able to find out. Look up at these cliffs and you can only think, no way. Eventually, the Park expanded and that was the end of cattle grazing here. We got a big day tomorrow, so let's sack out." With no objections, all was soon quiet except for the roar of the nearby Kings River.

The early morning glow, signaling the start of the third day, awoke Pablo. It would take over an hour longer to see the sun due to the straight-up cliffs on the east side of the valley. Looking over to the west, Pablo could see the bright sun rays starting their downward march from the tips of the high granite peaks. Clyde was already up, just completing the last step of putting a cup of cold water in the freshly brewed pot of coffee. Seeing his tent move and finally the zipper opening in the door and Pablo's head poke out, Clyde motioned for Pablo to get up. Pablo knew there was no way coffee was going to be served to him in bed like Clyde always did for Deb. After considerable flopping around in his tent, Pablo finally crawled out, stretched, and ambled over to the fire. The warm, comforting taste of the coffee along with the not-too-distant sound of the horses' bells signaling contented grazing always made this one of Pablo's favorite times of the day. The two clients have not moved a muscle yet, so Pablo knew he had plenty of time for a second cup.

Sitting on a rock, across the fire from Clyde, Pablo turned his gaze north, upcanyon toward the new day's journey. Clyde noticed this and started in. "Well, today is going to be interesting for you. First of all, since the bridge across this river was taken out during the flood after the 1996–97 winter, getting across will be a challenge. We'll have to stay on this side and go upstream first. Find a wide flat area to cross Goddard Creek. You remember me talking about Martha Lake below Goddard Peak. All that water flows north to the San Joaquin River. On this side of that peak, all the water flows south to the Kings River. This is where the two meet. We would never get across here, so it's the old adage of divide and conquer. We'll cross each separately. Most likely we'll have to keep the clients on their horses for it will be too deep and dangerous for them to cross on foot. They would be swept away for sure. Hopefully the horses will keep their footing through this.

"That is only the beginning. Then we get to do it all over again crossing the main channel of the river, but at least it will be minus all the water from Goddard. One good thing is

Hobbled horse with bell

we will be going up to the Pacific Crest Trail at the Palisade Creek, dropping the clients off, and returning to here. Therefore, we don't have to break our camp here. We'll take the empty packhorse with us. Don't want to leave Pearl here by herself. She would just follow us anyway."

The clients finally got up and started to pack their gear. Pablo went out with Clyde to retrieve the horses. All were contently standing in the morning sun with bellies full, waiting for the day to start. With hobbles removed they were led back to camp and the saddling began. The clients were stiff and sore, but knowing today would only be a half a day in the saddle, there was a slight spring in their step. Soon all was loaded up, the fire put out, and the group was on its way.

Leaving the old main trail, the cross-country ride on the left side of the river to Goddard Creek took about thirty minutes. Here Pablo noted the terrain changing. It started to look like high desert. Getting to the water's edge of Goddard Creek, Clyde paused only momentarily before starting in, with the clients following. His horse was soon belly deep. He changed course often to take advantage of the rock bars on the river bed in order to stay in the shallowest part of the channel. Pablo followed, pulling Diamond X, carrying the clients' gear, and the barebacked Pearl, who was last. Pablo could see the clients were white-knuckled. Their riding horses only slipped occasionally, just enough to let 'em know this was no cakewalk. Pablo kept a sharp eye on the clients, for in times like this their instinct was to jump off if the horse struggled a little. In most cases this would be a serious mistake. Always best to just stay centered on the horse and ride it out. The last thing a good mountain horse wants to do is fall down. Bailing off in this cold, deep, and swift water could be fatal.

The group continued and the opposite shore slowly approached. Clyde was first to pop out of the water and the clients soon followed, much to their relief. When all were safely on dry land, Clyde turned in the saddle and said with a slight smile, "That was just the warm up. In about ten minutes we get to cross the main channel of the Kings River. That will be a E ticket ride." Pablo knew Clyde was just having fun with the clients, but as they approached the river's edge, Pablo thought the clients were going to crap their pants. Without any hesitation, Clyde dove into the river, waving his right arm for all to follow. Even if the clients tried to protest, their voices would be lost to the river's roar, and the riding horses would follow Clyde anyway. The last thing Pablo did before entering the water was unsnap Pearl. Better to let her make her own way than to pull back and be a big problem for Diamond X.

Clyde changed course more often now, and with a strict voice instructed the clients to stay directly behind him and to not pull back on the reins. Let the horses have their heads. The group continued the serpentine course across as Clyde aimed for the opposite shore. The water was much swifter here, and Pablo often looked down and saw the deep underwater drop-off from the three-foot-deep bar they were on. Going in the deeper parts would certainly mean a desperate swim. Not a word came out of the clients. Pablo knew they were scared stiff, but they hung onto their saddle horns with both hands and stayed in the center of their saddles. Not having the added water from Goddard Creek was the only thing that made this crossing remotely possible.

Finally, Clyde popped up on the opposite shore, followed by the clients and then Pablo with the packhorses. All the animals had streams of water running down their legs and bellies but were immediately content to simply turn their attention to the nearest blade of grass and start to graze as if this was an everyday occurrence before breakfast. The clients suddenly became talkative, a sign they were greatly relieved the ordeal was over. Clyde didn't waste much time before continuing the short distance to the established park trail and starting up toward the day's destination.

Riding up the right side of the river, the land seemed to change, starting to look like what Pablo imagined Nevada would look like. Dry and open with clumps of purple sage. Soon the group came upon a four-foot diameter tree newly fallen directly across a steep and narrow part of the trail. Going around the bottom was not possible due to the river. Uphill was the only option. Clyde dismounted, and asked the clients to do the same. He then removed the bridles and tied them to the saddle horns. Motioning for the clients to climb over the tree as best they could, he explained that he would lead the horses around the tree base about fifty feet up the side of the hill. He knew the uprooted base area would have soft dirt and be dangerous for the riders. Up he went and the riderless horses followed without having to be led. Clyde lunged and jumped his horse up the hill, around the tip of the tree base, and almost had to butt slide his horse down the other side. But soon enough, all were back on the trail. With the clients remounted, the group continued their trek.

As they crossed the feeder creek that came out of Windy Canyon, Pablo marveled at the rock work done by the park trail crew. The water was allowed to fan out, starting from the uphill side, and disperse over the downhill side through a line of rock openings. This diffused the energy of the water and prevented downhill erosion. The water flowing through the openings reminded Pablo of castle ramparts. The base of the rock foundation was an easy twenty feet down, and the trail crew had positioned boulders the size of small cars to serve as trail anchor. How they got 'em in place Pablo could only guess. This looked like something the Romans would build. The sides of the trail were lined with medium-size rocks and the center was filled with three-quarter-inch-size rocks. All looked surprisingly equal in size. Pablo was thinking they were manufactured somewhere else and flown in by helicopter. Just then Clyde turned in his saddle and explained all the rock was quarried on site by hand and bucketed in place. He explained how seriously the park takes trail work, and that up ahead would be another example.

After a pleasant ride along the river's edge, the group came upon Cartridge Creek. Here was a bridge the size of which surprised Pablo. He wondered how these big timbers could be here and put into place high above the raging creek below. The bridge was elevated well above any high water level, thus safe from being washed out. It was so sturdy, Pablo thought a school bus could safely go over it. The timbered side rails gave comfort to the clients and kept the horses down the center. Thus, no problem.

The trail winded sidehill up the canyon and went over open slab granite. In one place the surface had enough of a pitch to it that Pablo got concerned as he looked ahead of Clyde. But when he got to that stretch of trail he noticed notches of the rock surface had been chipped out, creating toeholds for the horses. This gave him some comfort, knowing the horses at least had a chance to not slip off down the slab and into the river below. He was glad he left Pearl's lead rope unsnapped.

Clyde turned in the saddle and explained to the clients why the lead ropes on any pack string should be undone during these risky portions. "If one pulls back it could yank the entire string off balance and into the river. That's exactly what happened to a park trail crew packer a few years ago. The whole string of mules was pulled into the river and one drowned. He had to climb down into the cold raging river and try to save as many as he could. They were in water over their heads, with fully loaded packs and upside down. Pablo, never make that mistake. Always err on the side of caution and safety. Give these mountain animals the best chance of survival, for they are more able to take care of themselves than you might think. It's the same principle coming down or going up the ugly switchbacks we were on two days ago."

Then things really got scary. The solid rock trail came around a turn and Pablo could only see a solid granite wall. But Clyde didn't even slow down, and soon Pablo could see the trail was blasted out of the cliff. Going along this narrow ledge of a trail, the right side of the pack load would gently rub along the rock wall, and Pablo, looking back, could see the left pack sometimes hanging over the ledge on the left side of the trail. Looking down, it was an eighty-foot sheer drop-off into the raging river. Pablo silently thanked

Clyde for making the pack loads narrow, just for this purpose. Just as Pablo's nerves were starting to get to him, the string came out to a small clearing and into view came an awesome sight. The river dumped into a huge bowl of swirling water. There was a small rock flat next to its rim, where Clyde pulled up to a stop so the clients could dismount.

Clyde explained this was called the Devil's Washtub, and the reason was obvious. It was a swirling mass of water, just like in a washing machine. Not being able to see the bottom, one didn't want to get too close for to fall into that would not be fun. It was a great place for pictures, so they all stood for the photo op. Even the horses got into the scene and seemed to enjoy the attention. Clyde told everyone the trail from now on was a piece of cake. The clients were jubilant, for at last the pressure was off. They knew the end was in sight, just up the trail by no more than an hour.

Riding up to Palisade Creek at the junction where it dumps into the Kings River presented the group with completely differ-ent scenery. Suddenly the country took on a high Alpine character. Sighs of relief were expressed by the clients upon seeing the junction of the Pacific Crest Trail. Here they dismounted and the packhorse with their backpacks was unloaded. Group pictures, handshakes, and farewells were exchanged. The clients decided to camp at that location for the remaining part of the day and get an early start in the morning. Clyde and Pablo turned the string around and started the return trek. Part way back down the river trail, Clyde pointed off in the western sky. "Look at those thunder heads. We better not waste time on all this open rock. Don't want to get caught out here if lightening comes. Heavy rain won't make crossing over the slick rock or getting past both rivers any easier."

The pace picked up dramatically. The horses could sense the urgency and needed no encouragement. On the way back, Pablo still marveled at Devil's Washtub, this remarkable creation of nature. Going by the cliffs with their drop-offs didn't seem as scary this time. Moving along at a fast clip, they soon came upon the two river crossings, which they went through without even slowing down. Camp was a welcome sight, especially since it was already set up. Unsaddling and hobbling the horses so they could graze took only twenty minutes. Just as both of them sat down to enjoy the newly started fire, a gentle rain started. Thunder could be heard upcanyon, and soon flashes of lightning could be seen. Clyde just turned to Pablo and with a sly grin said, "Mother nature let us get by another day."

CHAPTER 5

Lower Indian Lake

The song birds were especially active this morning, awakening Pablo about 4:45 a.m. This gave him a few extra minutes to stretch after his five-day ride on the Tehipite trip. Looking out the bunkhouse window, he noticed Clyde coming down the stairs from the second story bedroom. He had his own cup of coffee, so Pablo knew he was returning from delivering Deb her morning cup. Walking past the window, Clyde lifted his cup and motioned for Pablo to go get his cup filled so the day could get started.

As Pablo walked out to the corral, Clyde met him with the first of the day's horses, and said, "We'll need five saddle horses for guests and another three for us. They also have another six people walking, so it's a large group for today. Taking 'em up to Lower Indian Lake in the Red Mountain Basin. Deb's going, and so will need seven packhorses for all the gear, theirs and ours."

Pablo helped Clyde pull out the saddle horses for the guests, Howdy, Trapper, Jigger, Little Shot, and Cloud. He then got the three guide horses, Jay, Harley, and Mesa. All the saddling work took them about thirty minutes. The horses were then loaded into the first trailer.

Next came the packhorses: Diamond X, Sundown, Pearl, Tobacco, Valor, Cinch, and Nevada. Pablo started putting on the pack saddles while Clyde retrieved the pack bags to preload the clients' gear. Since the clients were a little slow getting their camping equipment on the loading dock, Clyde loaded the guides' gear first. The last thing for that one load was the food box Deb was putting together in the cookhouse. Clyde called over to Pablo, saying, "Might want to get clothes for two nights. Since some of these horses have had a workout for the past five days, we'll spend a layover day up there. The horses would enjoy a day off in the high meadow grass."

Pablo was quietly thankful, even though he knew his enjoyment of a layover day wouldn't be any factor in Clyde's decision. To Clyde, the animals' comfort came before humans. Taking a short break from saddling, Pablo slipped back to his room and got an extra change of clothes and stuffed 'em in his overnight bag to be loaded. After finishing the last pack saddle, loading the seven horses into the second trailer went easy. In fact, the horses made it easy, having done this routine all their lives.

Finally, the clients rolled up with their gear piled high in the pickup bed. With it all transferred to the dock, Pablo couldn't believe how high the pile was. But somehow Clyde had it figured and was right on again. With all the prepacking done, there were seven evenly distributed horse loads. After loading all the gear into the flatbeds, the whole group was ready to roll out. They drove by the cookhouse, stopping to place the food container in the back, along with Dinkey. Then, with Deb driving the second rig, out the gate they went at 7:45 a.m.

The six-mile haul up to the Courtright Lake Maxon Trailhead was relaxing. Clyde had always felt that getting an early start was the secret to a good day. That way, you weren't in a hurry to catch up and could enjoy the small wonders you would normally overlook. Pablo had time to notice two grouse to his right, no more than five feet from the road edge. They gave him a casual glance and resumed pecking at the low buds hanging from the bushes. He then remembered the overactive songbirds early that morning, and felt today was going to be another good day.

Unloading the saddle horses at the spike station was first. Then came Deb's riding animal. Pablo knew this was so Deb could get the clients started right away. He and Clyde would then catch up later with the packhorses. As the six hikers of the group started out, Deb was fitting saddles to the leg lengths of the riders. With this done and radios checked, Deb led the riders out of the spike station and soon made the first turn and disappeared from sight.

Turning to the pile of stuffed pack bags, Pablo, Clyde, and even Dinkey gave a deep sigh as a signal to get started. After each packhorse was led out of the trailer, it was loaded, the top tarp placed, and the lash rope tied. The horse was then led to the other hitching rail and tied up. One by one, the horses were led out of the trailer, loaded up in similar fashion, and ultimately secured to the horse in front. Using this system, the whole seven-head string was loaded up, tied together, and ready to go in forty-five minutes. As they headed out, Clyde radioed up to Deb, letting her know the duo was on its way and asking how all was going. She replied they had only needed one pee stop so far, and that all the saddle cinches had been rechecked. With this info, Pablo, who was leading the string, relaxed and thought, "Yep, this is going to be a fine day."

After about thirty minutes, Clyde chimed in. "This is a nice group of fellows. All of them work as either city planners, chief financial officers, et cetera, from several cities up and down the Central California coast. They either knew each other as college students or through networking associations from work. They come up here about every other year and have a good time. The eager beavers like to walk and the others like to ride. That's OK. In the wilderness, there's something for everyone. The ride is about six hours, so the walkers came make it in one day if they hustle. They've done this before, so I'm not worried about 'em."

Going past the wilderness boundary sign, the string started up the switchbacks toward the Hobbler Lake turnoff. Pablo noticed the newly snapped off branches in the trail. He hadn't been up this trail in over a week, but, remembering a recent wind storm, realized the reason. Things change continuously in the high country and Mother Nature makes the rules. Not a cloud in the sky today though.

Heading downslope toward Long Meadow in a dense fir tree section, Pablo suddenly pulled his reins to stop his horse. Thirty feet in front of him was a young bear, stopped, and looking back over its right shoulder. Pablo pointed downtrail while turning to Clyde in the back. Just then Dinkey, who was trailing in the rear, bolted forward and Clyde hollered "STOP!" Dinkey, who by then was in full gear and up next to Pablo, skidded to a stop and returned back behind Clyde. Clyde calmly remarked to Pablo in the dead quiet of the forest, "Just let this young bear figure it out and decide to get off the trail and meander off. Don't want to scare him into running downtrail. Remember, Deb is up ahead with the riders. If that bear came running up from behind, it would surely spook all the riding animals and could easily get someone hurt."

After what seemed an eternity but in reality was only a few seconds, the bear lifted his nose back toward Pablo and then downtrail. Figuring horse and human smells were in both directions, he turned ninety degrees and headed straight into the forest. Within a few minutes all was calm and quiet. Clyde called up to Pablo, "Should be OK now, just take it easy. The horses might get a little jumpy when they get to the smell, but stay calm and don't worry."

Sure enough, as the group went by the bear's previous location, the horses got a little snorty and did a minor sidestep, but stayed in line, and soon the episode was forgotten. Even Dinkey, after crossing the bear's side trail, only gave a short pause while looking in the direction the bear had taken, then retook her position in the back behind Clyde's horse. Pablo had just learned another small lesson. Just stay cool and let the animal sort it out without your hooping and hollering. As Clyde told him last year, "Sometimes in life situations, you have to react with a hair trigger reflex, and other times it's best to take a deep breath and let things just sort themselves out. Wisdom is knowing the difference."

Within fifteen minutes, Pablo and Clyde caught up with Deb and her riders. They had stopped at Post Corral Meadow for a short rest. The hikers of the group had just left the site to resume their walk up the trail, knowing they had better keep moving since the riders had caught up to them.

They crossed Post Corral Creek and the bottom end of the meadow, where the trail started uphill toward Red Mountain Basin. Clyde remarked that he remembered this meadow being twice the size forty years ago, but lodgepole pines had slowly encroached from the sides. Within a few more decades, this meadow will only be a memory.

Continuing the assent, the group filed through the deep cut in the granite blasted out by a trail crew back in the sixties. This eliminated the open, flat, and angled slab the prior trail had to go over. However, during a heavy rain storm, the new route acted as a huge water trough. Sometimes the water would become a raging torrent down this alley. But having this cutout made it much safer in snow or ice.

After about forty-five minutes, the procession topped out at a location Clyde called the Niche, at about the 9,400 foot level. The trail pops out through the rocks to a nice flat zone. It's the last place one can see the Post Corral drainage and the first place to see Red Mountain Basin. And it's a good place to take a short rest. The group could see Red Mountain itself, as well as the saddle to the right

of the mountain that was Hell for Sure Pass. These views brought everything into perspective, and indicated the boundary of Kings Canyon National Park.

Continuing on, they passed Fleming Lake and started up the gradual incline toward Indian Lake. Pablo could now see Mount Henry. He was always fascinated by the accomplishments of some of the high Sierra predecessors, and remembered Clyde telling him that Joseph LeConte named the peak after Joseph Henry. Professor Henry was not only a professor at Princeton, but was instrumental in the creation of such organizations as the Smithsonian Institution, the National Academy of Sciences, and the US Weather Bureau.

As they went past the Rae Lake turnoff, Clyde pointed to the right and called up to Pablo, "Up there is a granite basin that contains Davis Lake. You remember I told ya it was named after George Davis, the USGS mapmaker. Well, this side of that rock bluff and down in the trees is a little meadow hideout where Stephanie Wright used to hang out. I told you last year I'd clue you in on her, so I guess I'm finally getting around to it.

"Stephanie is the daughter of Beatrice Wright. Bea is the lady I bought the station from back in 1980. Remember, she's the one buried next to my uncle Auggie down at the Academy Cemetery. Anyway, Stephanie sort of came along with the deal. She worked with me for several seasons and was a big help getting me started. Never wanted anything to do with the hour rides at Dinkey. Drew the line there. Packing in the high country was her only interest.

"I mentioned to ya last year about a paraplegic named Perko who wanted to get up to Bench Canyon. A safer route needed to be found, so Stephanie and Deb spent three days, full of torrential rains and lightning, scouting out a new route. It went up Meadow Brook Trail, then cut across to the regular Fall Creek Trail to finish up the way to Bench. This bypass cut almost an hour off of the time. More importantly, it was much safer and went over mostly granite. Thus there was little to no impact on the land. It also opens up to a view looking south and east that is breathtaking. All of this would have been missed without their efforts.

"During this venture, it was discovered that the old stock trail went that way. Ya can still see the old trail markers on some trees, as well as a couple cut out logs. It seems back in those days, the stock routes were always as high as they could get, for several reasons. They didn't have to be down along the main rivers where the spring flow would be a raging torrent, and the same for the side streams joining in. Getting across them with a large band of sheep or cattle herd could be lethal. Staying up high eliminated this trap, as the stream crossings up there are much smaller and the sun exposure melts off the snow faster.

"I have to give Stephanie Wright credit for not only the new route but that insight on history of the area. Ya, Stephanie is a colorful character. Her horses and mules were always giants. Seems they were all about seventeen hands high. Now you have to know, Stephanie herself was all of about five foot nothin'. She always had to get her horse next to or straddling a log that she could step up on and then climb into the saddle. How she was able to get the high top loads onto the pack mules and then tarp and tie everything is beyond me. Also, this is a woman who leads a mule string with two little rat-type dogs following along. I tell you Pablo, these dogs were rejects from the pound. They looked like dogs put together from a pile of spare parts. It takes a special type of person to see their beauty. Imagine coming upon this little lady with these dogs, mules in tow, and with the language from her booming voice that would turn the trees blue and make a sailor blush. Even her mule names were off-color. The most mild one was Hell-For-Sure. The names went way off after that. You get the picture.

"Steph was good friends with the pisser group I told you about last year. Needless to say, she enjoyed drinking along with them, so it was a perfect match. After her first trip with them, the group always asked if she could be their packer every year. They kept that up until the leader, who was a hopeless alcoholic, died at a relatively young age. It was reported by a strange, anonymous lady that he had passed away in a hotel room in his hometown."

Pablo looked back with a puzzled look on his face. "Porque es la hombre don un hotel proximo de su casa?"

"Well, Pablo," Clyde continued after a long sigh, "some day I'll spell it out for ya. Anyway, it seems this leader was quite well off financially, and I heard that at the funeral service the widow wasn't the least bit distraught. In fact, she seemed to have a smile the whole time."

Pablo again looked back with the same puzzled look and only replied, "Porque?"

After another long sigh, Clyde said, "Pablo, that also will take some explaining. You need to tighten up that third packhorse's lead rope. Getting a little loose. Ya don't want the fourth horse to step over it and create a wreck."

Pablo quickly stopped the string and took up the slack on the lead line, which wasn't that bad. He realized Clyde just didn't want to continue the explanation right now, so he dropped his questioning.

"Anyway, back to Stephanie," Clyde continued. "Her riding horses always seemed to be just short of fully trained. Often they were were what I call counterfeit. You know the type, Pablo—for no reason at all they would simply blow up and start bucking. Most disconcerting when you are trying to relax and enjoy the ride. Could never put a client on any of 'em. That trait is what finally did Stephanie in.

"On her way out one day with two clients, her riding horse suddenly went to bucking and threw her off, breaking her calcaneus, or heel, bone in the process. Somehow she made it back to the trailhead with the clients. It took a year to fully heal, and that was essentially the end of her working as a commercial packer. She later would pack herself in with the same rank horses, mules, and dogs and stay two weeks here, then move and stay another week or so there. Come out to resupply and go back in. Mostly to just sit, enjoy the scenery, and read. Now she doesn't even do that. Just trailers up her few remaining animals and camps out in an out-of-the-way spot off the Courtright road. When we go back to the station, maybe we'll stop by her camp and I'll introduce ya."

As the group was approaching their destination of Lower Indian Lake, Pablo could see the last rider of the string of saddle horses with Deb. Perfect timing again, he thought—caught up to 'em just as all reach camp.

As usual, all three assisted in getting the clients off their horses first. This was mainly for safety and because of the clients being anxious to get off due to sore butts. Sometimes they would try to get off themselves and, being tired and out of shape, it could lead to a big problem, especially if a foot got hung up in a stirrup. Telling folks to not get off until they had help from one of the guides was always a must. Pablo never heard any client object to the rule.

With this done and their gear unloaded, Pablo and Clyde started repacking the empty pack bags with the ropes and tarps. After doubling up on the empties, only half the packhorses were loaded for the short ride to the packer camp. Pablo remembered it was Clyde's policy to never camp with the clients or next to any lake, in order to avoid having the horses disturb them or the water. They would return the short distance to Fleming Meadow, an out of the way hideout camp that the horses seemed to like and would not wander from during the night.

Sitting by a small fire that evening, after Deb had made an early exit to the sleeping bag, Pablo's mind wandered back to Stephanie Wright. He had heard her name several times in various places and couldn't shake her loose from his thoughts. Finally, he gave in and asked Clyde, "Can you tell me more about Stephanie? You and Deb have mentioned her several times."

Clyde took a deep breath and started in. "Well, I've been told in high school she was a valedictorian. Never thought college would be of any value to her. She just wanted to be with her horses and mules, and here in the mountains. Ya, at times her language gets out of hand, she can drink a little too much, and generally has a lot of bark on her, so to speak. Always seems to make poor choices in husbands and boyfriends. However, she is a kind soul, almost to a fault. Her word is solid. If I asked her to do something, she would kill herself getting it done, no matter what. I've learned a heck of a lot from her on the nooks and crannies in these hills. Out of the way places all others would just ride or walk by.

"She is a great example of a person not to be judged by her exterior. Sit down, ask the occasional question, and just simply listen. Pablo, in life, you never really know where the pearls of wisdom will come from. Most of the time, ya don't realize it until much later after the fact. She is a wealth of knowledge as to horse routes that are possible into out of the way places. Prejudging and discounting someone like her is a mistake.

"This reminds me of a statement I once heard: 'The single biggest thing that inhibits success is intellectual arrogance.' Read that from the sixth-richest man in the world, Warren Buffet. If I had to just rely on educated guesses, it would have taken much longer to learn this country. Doing advance homework is a critical time-saver. It can mean the difference between success and a total waste of valuable time. That's another thing to glean from this. Your most valuable asset in life isn't money, things, or status, but time. Time management is everything. The more you can learn and grow in the least amount of time is what being prosperous and successful is all about.

"The endpoint is only a target, the getting there is what life is all about. So, along your way, learn from anybody and everybody. Don't be in a hurry to prejudge your source. Take the minutes to ask the extra question, then another. Trust me, it's time well spent. It may seem slow, but just like I told ya about the horse pack trip, the fastest way to your destination is slowly, because you're paying attention to the details. First thing ya know, your are at the end of the day's trail and it's early. I mean in the day and in life. Gives you more time to pursue new goals."

Looking up, Pablo noticed the evening sun's shadow creeping up the granite mountainsides. The still-lit area changed to a bright orange that he never got tired of. This was the Alpine Glow Clyde had told him about at the beginning of last summer. He never got tired of the view or of the wonder of its creation. Often, a long study session in college would leave him all tied up in knots and he had trouble relaxing into sleep. But by putting the vision of the Alpine Glow in his head, he would suddenly find himself relaxing and drifting off.

Next morning, with one eye slightly cracked open, Pablo could see through the bug netting of his small tent, the premorning glow high on the granite peaks above their little camp. It would be a good hour before full sunup. No need to jump up. The Clydes hadn't stirred yet. Lying back with both eyes open now, Pablo took a deep breath and just listened. Off in the distance, he could hear the faint sounds of the bells on the hobbled horses. This was always the first thing he listened for in the morning. Upon hearing them, he knew they hadn't wandered far over the night and that the day was off to a good start. More so, with the only occasional ringing, they weren't on the move, just relaxing with full bellies. That's the sound Clyde always said was good—they're full from grazing, rested, and just standing around, no doubt, talking politics.

Tuning his ears to new sounds, Pablo heard the first morning sounds of the finches and nuthatches. As their tempo and frequency increased, it was in direct sequence with the gradual increase of daylight. The background music to this whole symphony was the sound of flowing water in nearby Fleming Creek. Suddenly, one of the small finches fluttered to a rest on an extended lodgepole branch no more than one foot from his head, just outside the tent netting. It jumped around, somewhat nervously, but never stopped staring down directly at Pablo. Pablo didn't move a muscle, wanting to see who would flinch first. The contest went on for what seemed like hours, but really was only seconds. Finally, Pablo involuntarily blinked. That's all it took. The finch fled as if the branch had suddenly gotten hot.

Not long after that, Pablo could hear Clyde getting up, no doubt getting coffee started, always his first priority in the morning. Deb was still sound asleep. Using a small one-burner stove, the coffee was ready in about fifteen minutes. Before the drought induced fire closures in the wilderness, Clyde had always used an open campfire. Having to use stoves out of necessity during this time, he came to appreciate how much faster they were and stuck with 'em, even after the fire ban was lifted. Pablo could easily see why. Whenever Clyde did make an open fire, it was a time-consuming endeavor. First, he dug a small hole, about one foot long by one foot deep. Then he had to go out and forage for wood. After getting it started, he would place a grate over the hole and put pots on that. After all the cooking and heating was done, he would fill the hole with water to ensure all the embers were put out. After all the water settled into the ground, he would then backfill the hole with the same dirt and finally sprinkle some natural pine needle vegetation over the whole site. One would never know there was ever a fire there. He never blackened any rocks either. But, all this took time, blackened the pots, and meant he had to pack a fire grate. Life has been much easier with the small stove.

SUGAR PINE

Claudia Fletcher
2020

Pablo could smell the coffee before being called. Clyde motioned for him to help himself as he headed back to his tent, delivering Deb's full, steaming cup. He then joined Pablo, sitting around the camp waiting for the sun to finish rising. "No big reason to load up this fine morning and head out," Clyde declared. "Could do a layover day and go exploring. Thought you might like to see Upper Indian Lake. We could just take our saddle horses. The rest of the herd isn't going anywhere. They could use a day of relaxation anyway."

This was music to Pablo's ears. Deb chimed in with, "You boys go right ahead, I've been there many times. Just sitting down and reading a book sounds good to me." So, after a quick breakfast of premade homemade burritos, the two went out to retrieve their saddle horses.

There is always a method to approaching a hobbled horse herd. The duo made a wide circle around to the back of the group. This almost always required going uphill to get behind 'em. This way, if the group spooked for any reason, they would be hopping toward camp. Though this rarely happened, it is always good to plan ahead. Jay and Harley stood like statues, never flinching while the lead ropes were attached and the hobbles removed. Even better, as the two horses were led away, none of the others followed. All were content to stay right where they were. Clyde quietly replied, "Yep, the day just keeps getting better."

After saddling the horses and saying goodbye to Deb, all turned on their radios. This was to keep an open communication with Deb, if needed. Safety for all comes first. Up the trail the duo marched, with Dinkey following. She was always eager to go on any outing. In fact, tying her up would have been the only other option. As they went by the large, flat meadow that surrounds Lower Indian Lake, they both noticed two of the previous day's clients out for an early contest with the lake's trout. Pablo noticed they already had three nice fish and big grins. After passing, Clyde softly spoke up to Pablo. "Seeing them enjoy themselves up here in this high

Alpine setting never gets old. I've been enjoying that reaction for forty years and still feel as good about it as the first time."

After getting around to the backside of the lake and large meadow, the trail started up through a steep gorge, and soon fed through a narrow gap with high granite walls on both sides. The footing was treacherous as it was all broken rock and several high steps that meant jump-ups for the horses. Pablo stopped short and turned around to Clyde with a questioning look. He only received a blank stare from Clyde, who was wearing a slight smile. Pablo turned his attention back uptrail, then turned to Clyde again, only to get the same reaction.

Clyde finally spoke up. "Well, what is your thought process telling you?"

Pablo took a deep breath and stated, "Us riding up this would put the horses at a disadvantage. Our weight could cause 'em to stumble and go down on their knees. This would cause them to have to start scrambling. If that happened, they could easily slam into the granite wall on either side and cause us to bang up a knee or ankle. So, I think it's better we get off and slowly walk the horses up this part."

With this, Clyde's immediate reaction was a big smile. "Good thinking. Always better to avoid a problem then have to deal with it later. Remember, taking calculated risks is OK, but taking unnecessary chances is never wise. Checking your ego and playing it safe when you have the option is not only smart, but you tend to live longer."

After walking up through this part, which turned to only be about thirty yards, the two remounted and finished the journey to Upper Indian Lake. They tied up the horses in a rocky area prior to the lake shore. Clyde then motioned for Pablo to wander around to the backside of the lake.

On the way, Pablo couldn't help but notice the number of large fish clearly visible just under the water's surface. All seemed to be in the twelve- to fourteen-inch category. From the backside, or north end, of the lake, Pablo looked south and his jaw dropped at the view. He felt he was truly at the top of the world here above the tree line. He remembered Clyde telling him last year how all the water flowing south went into the Kings River. Behind him all the water flowed to the San Joaquin River. He remembered being told last year that Mosquito Pass was a little to the west of him.

Suddenly, he had to grab his hat, as the wind almost blew it to the next county. Yep, that wind tunnel effect Clyde talked about last year was definitely present here. He laughed, recalling the "putting rocks in your pockets" idea to keep from blowing away. Right now, it actually seemed like a good idea. Looking over the north edge, he could see the whole San Joaquin River drainage. Over the winter, he had read that the series of hydroelectric plants put in by Edison Company many decades ago down this drainage made this river the hardest working water in the world. From way up here, he could easily see why.

Hiking back around the lake, Pablo found Clyde stretched out on a warm, sunny rock with his hat covering his face. Dinkey was lying at his side, her head on his lap. Both were fast asleep, but they came awake after Pablo stepped on some loose, decomposed granite. Tipping his hat back, Clyde simply said, "After your connection with a true natural wonder, ya must be getting hungry. What do you say we head back down and help Deb make dinner."

That sounded good to Pablo. Off they went toward camp. Coming to the narrow chute, Pablo and Clyde again dismounted and walked their horses down, then remounted and continued.

Back at camp, Pablo couldn't stop telling Deb about the sights he experienced from his being on top of the world. His chatter continued the next day, all the way to the trailhead. Clyde was able to quiet him down some with the unloading of the gear, and the unsaddling and loading of all the horses into the trailers so they could head back to the pack station. However, Clyde noticed, Pablo never stopped grinning the whole way.

Down a cliff trail

CHAPTER 6

Uncommon Courage

Pablo was already up getting coffee when Clyde came in the back door returning from Deb's delivery. After he finished filling his cup, Pablo turned to Clyde asking, "What's up for today?"

After a deep sigh, Clyde responded. "Well, we are off to a big five-day outing. You remember that canyoneer group lead by Rick Ianniello we took in last year? They went down Blue Creek Canyon, which had never been done before. He also has gone down Crown Creek. Both trips ended up in Tehipite Valley. It was a first for each of those locations. Well, this time he's back with a new group of friends and they want to do both in the same trip.

"Ya, we take their gear to the bottom of Blue Canyon Valley, where the river exists. They're going to rappel down the next day to the valley. We'll come back around and go down the switchbacks and meet them down there. Then they want to hike back up those miserable switchbacks and do it all again down Crown Creek to the valley. Not only have these routes been done only once, by Rick himself, but this time both are going to be attempted on the same trip. Talk about a butt kicker!

"They originally wanted to schedule just four days to do all this, but I talked 'em into a five-day trip. We plan to use the middle day to rest up. He was reluctant at first, but finally agreed, especially after I informed him this would give me time to transport their climbing gear back up the switchbacks for the second attempt. I assured him, in the end, he'll be most thankful. It's a large group of eight people. All have extensive experience, so we'll see. Odds are someone will get hurt on this trip, but not if these individuals are truly experienced and pay strict attention to safety. I think if any group can do it, this one can.

"Rappelling down a cliff is much harder than climbing up. Once you commit to going down a sheer rock face and pull your ropes from the anchors, you're definitely committed. There's no going back up. Added to this is that they'll be doing it going down a waterfall; it's all done against a sheer rock wall with water pounding on you from above. In this situation, even a helicopter will have trouble getting to you. That takes professionalism, courage, and guts. Plus, they have do it all safely and then repeat it all two days later on the next canyon. If they can pull this off, it will be a first and one for the history books.

"So, let's refill our cups and get to work. The group came in late last night and is still sacked out. No problem, they're walking anyway. Because there are no riders, Deb gets to sit this one out. I don't think she's too distraught. Going up and down those hot, miserable switchbacks twice to that hole called Tehipite, dodging rattlesnakes and poison oak the whole way, is not exactly on her wish list. So," Clyde said with a grin, slapping Pablo on the back, "I'm sure glad you volunteered."

Pablo took a big gulp, minus the coffee, and followed Clyde out the back door. He knew this would be the most challenging trip he had yet made. He had to remind himself of what Clyde always said, "Take it slow, careful, and well-thought out, throw in some luck, and you just might make it through alive."

Pulling out the horses took some thought. Only the top-shelf A team was to go. This trip would not only test their narrow and steep trail agility, but to do so twice with only a one-day rest in between was going to test their conditioning. He felt confident in Jay, and Clyde motioned to get Jigger for him. Jigger was the type of horse best suited for this assignment. One of his best points was that Clyde could stop him, jump out of the saddle and leave the lead rope on the ground, and Jigger would never move a muscle. This allowed Clyde to quickly get back to any problem another horse may have and not worry about the whole string moving if the lead horse decided to walk off. Rarely, on this trail, was there anything to conveniently tie off to if you had to act fast. On the cliffside, taking care of a minor problem quickly, before a major wreck occurred, could mean the difference between life or death to the animals, and possibly to yourself as well.

String of horses

Pablo figured they would need seven packhorses to accommodate all the climbers' camping and heavy mountaineering gear, plus one horse for his and Clyde's gear. Out came Diamond X, Pearl, Nevada, July, Tobacco, Sundown, and Loper. Nevada was always a must for a trip like this. The other horses were bays or sorrels, but he was a black and white paint, easy to notice and perfect for the back of the string. With one glance, seeing him tells you all others are present and accounted for. This is especially helpful when night riding. Most of the time ya don't need a flashlight to see him on a switchback.

Halfway through the saddling, Rick, the leader, came over to check in and say hi. Pablo remembered him from last year. They went over the usual instructions, politely advising all to have their gear on the loading dock by 7:00 a.m. After looking over at the camp and not seeing any movement, Pablo asked if Rick needed any help. Rick replied all was good and he would get 'em going. Rick was astute enough to know Pablo still had enough work to do with the saddling and loading of the stock and didn't want Clyde to do it all.

As the group came to life and started unloading gear on the dock, Pablo noticed they were moving a little slow. No explanation was necessary. He remembered hearing partying voices until he fell asleep and knew it didn't stop then. Oh well, that much less booze they would have to haul. He was just glad they were not riding horses, and thus he would not be responsible for them and their woozy, throbbing heads for most of the day. He felt sorry for 'em though, having to walk all day in this altitude in that condition. But, choices have consequences, and they were young and mostly likely would survive.

After loading the horses in the trailer, work began on preparing the gear, which was all assembled by then. Yep, after all was bagged and ready to load, seven packhorses would be just right. That made fourteen side bags. Half went into the flatbed with the trailer and the other half went into Deb's truck. She would accompany them to the trailhead and help load. This was after she made breakfast, prepared four dinners, four breakfasts, and five lunches for the duo's five-day trip. With the walkers' vehicles out the front gate and on their way, Clyde's two vehicles rolled out, leaving Dinkey behind, since they were going into the national park and thus no dogs were allowed. Driving out, Dinkey looked sad sitting on the porch, but those are Park Service rules made by humans. Pablo was sure no dogs had input on that decision.

At the trailhead, with all the gear prepacked, the loading of the pack string only took the trio about forty-five minutes. Deb gave Pablo a hug and Clyde a kiss and off they went down the trail. Pablo always felt good after the first fifteen minutes of a ride. This gave him time to make sure all the loads were riding well, with no tilts. He had four packhorses in his string and Clyde followed with the other three.

The birds were out in full force. They provided a lot of noise and general commotion in the tree branches on both sides of the trail. Yep, the day was off to a good start and Pablo was able to relax. Coming across two deer grazing about forty yards to his right, he slowed down just a little. The deer looked up, but only had twitching noses, flipping ears, and wagging tails as they continued to chew, never moving their feet. Obviously they felt no threat from the moving string. Pablo knew if he came to a complete stop, they would panic and bolt. Keeping it moving slow and smooth was always best. Yep, he thought, the day was definitely off to a good start.

After about two miles down the trail and after two stream crossings, Pablo came to a situation that his reflexes made him suddenly pull back on the reins and signal Jay to slam on the brakes. This brought the whole string to a halt. Up ahead about forty feet and up a small tree just to the left of the trail perched two small bear cubs. The young lodgepole sagged with their weight and leaned toward the trail. At this spot, the trail had a steep hillside on the left and a sharp drop-off to the right. No way to get around. The horses hadn't noticed anything and were quietly grazing on the tall grass within easy reach to their left on the uphill side. Pablo turned in the saddle to Clyde with a questioning look.

Clyde just smiled and said, "Keep looking. Remember this same type of situation the other time with the bear running down the trail. Well, use the same thought process."

Pablo turned back straight in the saddle and reevaluated the situation. Those cubs weren't up that tree for no reason. The mother had ordered 'em up when she heard the string coming. So, where was the mother? Looking to the left, then to the right, Pablo saw nothing. Finally, a small flicker of movement caught his eye about fifty feet to his right under some low hanging branches. Pablo kept staring and sure enough, the mother bear's outline came into view. Now what? Well, he couldn't go around, since there was no way up or down from the trail. If he kicked his horse and charged right on through, that would put him and the string right between the cubs and the mother. Not a good idea. He glanced back and out of the corner of his eye he could see the horses still contently grazing. None of them had yet noticed the bears. Pablo then thought about the prior encounter, even though the situation was different, and decided he should approach it the same way. Relax, stay still, and let things work themselves out.

After what seemed an eternity, but was only about one minute, the mother gave a low grunt and the two cubs started their descent. Slowly at first, but with each not wanting to be left behind it soon became a scramble. On the ground they both plopped and scampered off across the trail and up to momma. The trio then turned and continued their downhill trek. Letting ample time lapse for them to get completely out of the area, Pablo finally nudged Jay forward, feeling good the horses never noticed the commotion. Approaching the crossing, Clyde called up, "Don't get too relaxed. Even though the horses didn't see the bears, they will definitely know they are around as soon as we cross the trail, so be ready."

Sure enough, as soon as Jay hit where the bears had crossed the trail, his nose went into overtime and he started to snort and jump sideways big time. This got the whole string in a somewhat uproar. Pablo had been ready for this. He hit Jay with both heels and got things moving fast. He felt the best solution was to keep the horses busy with going forward. Their instinct was to flee and he wanted this to be down the trail. It worked, all took off on a trot, in line down the middle of the trail. This went on for about fifty yards and Pablo started to gradually slow all of 'em down until a quiet walk was restored. Some snorting continued for a short while, but soon the horses realized they were out of their perceived danger. Pablo gave a deep sigh and turned back to Clyde, who was only smiling. No words needed to be said. Job well done.

At about the three hour mark, the duo came upon Crown Valley. Pablo always marveled at the row of old log cabins on this private land inholding. The trail is a public easement and to get off would be trespassing. Pablo had always been allowed over for a friendly chat with the owners. Whenever he stopped, it would only be when he didn't have clients. He never wanted to cause the crowd to descend on their private life. Also, he would tie up his string on the trail, so as not to create a stock trail down to the cabins. This all was a gesture of respect to the owners. This time he merely waved to the occupants as the string slowly passed.

At this point, Pablo and Clyde entered the Tehipite Forest Fire burn area. The fire happened about eight years earlier, and all the dead standing trees were starting to fall. Clyde had told him he used to hear two to three trees fall each season, and it was quite a treat. Now they could hear two to three fall a day, and it could get quite nerve-wracking. If one came down on your string or, worse, yourself, all heck would break loose. After any fire, dead standing trees posed a hazard for the next fifteen years. The combination of all the dead trees on the ground and the total coverage of the area with buck brush created another fuel load problem, just lying in wait for the next fire to start. This repeat of a fire every twenty years might make a healthy forest in the end, but it would take fifty to one hundred years to accomplish. The Forest Service's obsession with putting all fires out ASAP only added to the problem. Clyde felt structure protection and controlled burns should be the main focus when it came to fighting forest fires; however, in a wilderness zone this gets complicated.

Descending down a mountain grade to Crown Creek, the duo came upon the canyoneer group resting at the creekside. After watering the horses during the crossing, Pablo and Clyde had a chance to stop and chat with the nine adventurers. Pablo learned their names were Daniel Elson, Amanda Guenther, Alex Johnson, Julien Lecorps, Herve Mazoyer, Kevin Smith, "Jarro" Matthew Jaroslawski, "Nessa" Nessaroses Schear, and the leader, Rick Ianniello. Rick was the quiet type, but everyone seemed to respect him as the clear leader. Apparently he was quite well known in this sport around the nation.

After a short rest, which included eating lunch, the duo waved bye and headed up the mountain trail and onto Kettle Ridge. This was steep country and required multiple switchbacks through a burn area. The tree trunks were blackened and left their marks on the white pack tarps as the animals brushed by. After passing the Kings Canyon Park Boundary sign, Pablo came to a turn in the trail with a four-foot-diameter dead tree fallen across, blocking his route. All progress came to a stop. They tied up their riding horses and dallied the lead packhorse's rope to the saddle horns. This kept the whole string under control while the duo explored an alternate route.

High brush and downed trees blocked most options, but Clyde figured a route that might work. He then motioned for Pablo to follow him. After a few yards, Clyde stopped and unsnapped all the packhorses from each other, motioning for Pablo to do the same. Jumping over deadfall was extremely hazardous and having the horses tied together would guarantee a wreck. When Clyde remounted and resumed his progress, Pablo stepped his horse aside to let his loose string follow Clyde's. He then took up the rear. This allowed all seven packhorses to be together, which enhanced their comfort level.

As the group wound its way back and forth off-trail, the third packhorse gently rubbed against an eight-inch-diameter dead fir tree, which started to sway back and forth. Pablo saw this and knew it would be trouble. Just as he was about to holler up to Clyde, the inevitable happened. That tree came crashing down right on top of the fifth packhorse's pack, and the rodeo started. The uprooted tree was balancing across the horse's load and going back and forth like a see-saw, not wanting to get off. Clyde had been looking back and saw it all unfold. Kicking Jigger in the sides, Clyde leaped forward, followed by the string, the last four of which were bucking up a storm by then. Suddenly the tree came off the horse and was tumbling in the air, forcing Pablo to take a hard left turn to avoid getting hit. Pablo felt sure Clyde was going to be trampled. But after less than thirty yards the whole string slowed down and loosely gathered around Clyde before finally standing still, including the last horse, which had the confrontation with the tree. All were OK.

Clyde calmly looked back at Pablo and called, "Looks like we lived through that." Pablo answered with a dry mouth, "Ya, but I'll never know how." Clyde just shrugged his shoulders, turned his riding horse uptrail, and the whole loose string got in line voluntarily in the exact same order they started in. Pablo was amazed to watch as each horse waited for the other to get in the proper order. At the next flat area, Clyde pulled over to let Pablo resume the lead and reconnect the string. Pablo was still shook up. Having a

tree fall across a horse and not want to come off, causing a bucking rodeo, was nothing he had ever thought of, let alone actually seen or been through. He felt glad he brought an extra pair of underwear, knowing for sure he was going to need 'em after this. Looking back, Pablo noticed Clyde smiling and observing the surrounding wildlife as if nothing ever happened.

As the group topped Kettle Ridge, the granite monuments on the left were so close one could almost touch them. A short rest stop at the top gave the horses and Pablo a much needed break. The view was to die for. Looking north, east, and south, Pablo got the whole impact of the Middle Fork of the Kings River Canyon. He could easily see the reasoning that from the top of Spanish Mountain to the bottom of the downstream gorge, this area was deeper than the Grand Canyon. No questioning that fact from this vantage point.

The hiking group was still far behind back down the trail. Knowing it would take several hours for them to catch up, Pablo knew he could relax and not have to push for the remaining part of the trip. A small stream with an inviting meadow on both sides greeted them as they started their descent. It was a good place to water the horses, only big enough for one horse at a time to drink, but time was not an issue. After the last animal got its fill, Clyde called up to Pablo, "This area looks pleasant for an overnight stay, but don't. It's way too small and sensitive of a riparian area for that. The stock won't stay here anyway . . . not enough room, and I guarantee they will roam. By morning they will be off down either side of the mountain. Not a good way to start your day. Remember, any overnight site with stock has to have all the right components. If you forget one, you'll learn a hard lesson."

Pablo nodded his head, turned back straight in the saddle, nudged Jay, and proceeded down the backside of the mountain. The species of trees changed. The trail switchbacked around numerous extremely large red fir trees, mostly following the same drainage, only occasionally changing over to the next. The trail got steeper and the turns got tighter as the duo descended. They could hear the roar of Blue Canyon Creek getting louder as they progressed. Finally, upon reaching the creekside, the trail turned to follow the creek upcanyon. Clyde called out, "Hold up at the next wide spot. This is where we unload all their gear. Not much here but they don't care since it's only a jump-off point for them. This is the same place Rick chose last time."

RED FIR

Offloading the six pack-horses went easy. Their gear was well packed, each load in waterproof containers. Several were heavy, as mountaineering gear generally is. Soon, all the empty pack bags were reloaded onto the horses and off the duo went, uptrail to find a suitable campsite for the outfit. Pablo, in the lead, knew Clyde had a place in mind but didn't want to ask since he knew the answer would be, "Figure it out."

Within fifteen minutes they came to a somewhat wider place in the canyon. The horses had a route to get to water and enough grazing for one night, and there was a reasonable campsite for them the barely legal distance from the trail and water. Pablo stopped the string, turned in the saddle to Clyde, and only got a smile and nod in response. Yep, he felt, this will do.

Unloading the seventh packhorse with their gear only took a few minutes. After unsaddling, hobbling, and turning the horses out for the night's grazing, the duo could then get to making their own camp for the night. With tents up and sleeping bags inside, they cooked their dinner over the one-burner stove and called it a night early. Lying in his sleeping bag and trying to read his book, Pablo could only get past three pages before the rhythmic sounds of the loud creek gently rocked him off to sleep.

A clanking sound, easily heard over the creek noise, awoke Pablo. It was barely light and he could see Clyde pouring a cup of coffee he had already made. Clyde, noticing the rustle in Pablo's tent, called out, "Thought you were going to sleep all morning. It's already five o'clock and we're burning daylight."

Lying back in his bag trying to finish waking up, Pablo could hear the morning music familiar to all packers, the soft, faint sounds of the horses' bells a relatively short distance away. Yes, the day was again off to a good start. After two cups of coffee and a warmed breakfast egg burrito, Clyde and Pablo retrieved the nine lead ropes and calmly walked off into the predawn light to gather up the horses.

They then headed the saddled-up string the short stretch back down the trail to retrieve the loads from the group. The horses' bellies were full and all were well rested. Upon arrival at the prior afternoon's drop-off point, all the gear was neatly lined up for the pickup and all the people were gone. "Well, they're off," Clyde observed, "and I hope God watches over them." Heading back up the mountain wasn't as bad because the loads were minus the heavy climbing gear. The duo soon topped over Kettle Ridge and headed back down the west side. Crossing Crown Creek, they stopped only long enough to water the horses again. Turning to a new trail after passing Crown Valley, the group headed south toward Tehipite Valley.

Pablo again got a knot in his stomach when they got to the rim and looked down into the river gorge. Clyde was in the lead by then, and all seven packhorses were loose led when Clyde dropped out of sight over the edge. Pablo went past the Jesse Ray Hedgepath brass USGS benchmark and, with no hesitation, followed the last horse over. Down they went, with no time to rethink or second guess. Pablo figured Clyde did this on purpose.

They descended, occasionally kicking rocks down, which Clyde dodged because he was in front and thus downhill. It was tricky work, hard on the mind and the body. Just keep going and don't look down was the advice from Clyde that keep ringing in Pablo's head. Down,

Benchmark

down, the steady march continued, each horse picking its own way but staying on the trail, since there was no other option. Only after hitting the bottom did Pablo feel he could take his first deep breath, even though it had been a two-hour ride down.

Following along the Middle Fork of the Kings River was quite pleasant. Soon the duo came to an open valley with only sand, cactus, some sparse grass, and a magnificent view of Tehipite Dome. Clyde called back to Pablo, "Let's unload their gear over at that nice camp. It's got a good view of the Dome and has a breeze which helps keep the bugs away. As for us, we can camp over toward the inlet of Crown Creek. This gives them some privacy."

The canyoneers didn't get in until almost dark, carrying their climbing gear and dragging their butts. Tough day, but their descent down Blue Canyon Creek drainage was successful and no one had been injured. Needless to say, Rick spoke for the group of being thankful for Clyde's suggestion to have a layover day to rest up for the second descent through the Crown Creek drainage.

Day three was a lazy wake-up. Nobody was in a hurry. After coffee, Clyde called over to Pablo and said, "I think I figured out where the Native American pictographs are. Shouldn't take too long and it might be fun."

Off the duo went, while the canyoneers hadn't even gotten out of their tents yet. Crossing Crown Creek took some rock hopping.

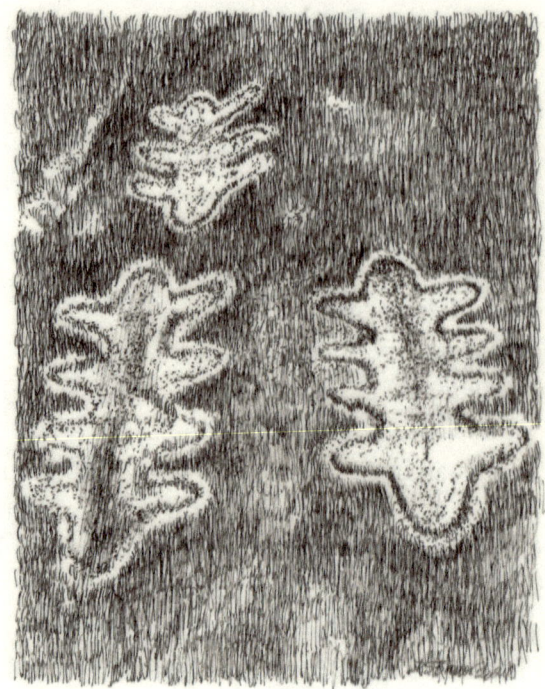

INDIAN PICTOGRAPHS
ON GRANITE ROCK

After following up the trail a short way, Clyde stopped and pointed to the right, off-trail. After picking their way around downed trees and over rocks, they suddenly came upon a small cave, basically a natural rock boulder that created a protective area underneath. When one sat on the ground in this small area, a smaller, smooth rock gave a perfect backrest. Right up above, at perfect arm's length, were three figures, chipped out of the rock directly facing down at the angle of the rock. Pablo scratched his head as to what it was a picture of. Since there was only room for one person, Clyde wasn't close to ask. He kept staring, but the meaning of the image wouldn't come to him. Clyde stood outside and only chuckled. "Pablo," he said, "you're trying too hard." That's when Pablo turned and Clyde handed him a perfectly formed oak leaf. These were on the ground by the thousands. Holding the leaf up to the images, the simplicity dawned on him and he felt embarrassed. Clyde chuckled and said,

"Don't worry, it happens to all of us from time to time. Let's get back and check the horses."

After checking all the stock, Pablo felt he could relax the remainder of the day. Clyde spoke up, "Go ahead and get a nap, because this early evening, when the temperature drops, we're heading back up the switchbacks with their climbing gear, dropping it off, and coming back down tonight in the dark." Clyde could see the horrified look on Pablo's face. He only chuckled and said, "Sounds fun, doesn't it?"

There was no way Pablo could sleep, but it didn't stop Clyde from napping. He awoke about 4 p.m. and said, "Time to saddle up."

Leaving with three loaded packhorses, since only the climbing gear was to be transported, the duo started the climb back up the cliff trail. The four remaining packhorses were left alone. Clyde said, "No need to tie 'em up. When they see us head up, that will change their minds about following." Sure enough, not one of the remaining animals choose to make even a step toward following. On the way up, Clyde called back, "Doing this now is necessary because it's cooler, and allows the horses to get a rest day tomorrow for the following day's trip out. The same for you."

After topping out at the rim, Pablo resisted the urge to stop, get off, and kiss the brass benchmark. No time for that, especially knowing he would only be turning around and going back down. After unloading the climbing gear at Gnat Meadow, the group turned and started their descent again. It was just getting full on dark, but the moon was out and gave a spooky glow to the cliffside. Down they went. Pablo could not see much, just an occasional glimpse of the horse's butt in front of him. This comfort only lasted seconds before the animal disappeared from view, and he could only trust his riding horse. Clyde, out in front, never turned on his headlamp the whole way down. Hearing the noise of the river getting louder only gave small comfort, as he had to admit he was scared stiff the whole way down. The horses never even noticed. They were glad to be on the way back to their buddies. Upon reaching the camp, everyone was in their tents and asleep except one, Daniel, who stuck his head out and said something like, "I can't believe you made it back tonight and alive at that." Pablo didn't respond, but quietly admitted he felt the same way.

The sun was well above the canyon rim when Pablo awoke. It was past seven and Clyde had been up for a couple of hours. Clyde called over to Pablo, "About time. Thought I was gonna have to drink this whole pot of coffee myself." Pablo shook his head a couple of times to get further awake. Remembering the previous night's ride, his whole body shook. He figured he better get up before everything got cold.

He sat next to the fire and looked up Crown Creek Canyon, just to the left of Tehipite Dome, thinking not a grander sight could be had. Clyde pointed up the sheer rock walls with water tumbling down and said, "This is a ringside seat to the show. Those guys will be coming down those cliffs, on ropes, in the water, and all you have to do is sit back and watch. Hope they don't fall, for they might bounce all the way to this camp and we'd have to jump out of the way. So, stay on your toes."

Late afternoon, Pablo could see the first of the group collecting at the top of a waterfall cliff. He knew there were many others up the canyon, but this was the first one in his view. The whole group was assembled at the top edge of the rock wall. With binoculars he could count nine people. Good, the whole group made it this far, he thought.

After what seemed like an eternity, a long rope was thrown off the edge, right in the middle of the waterfall. It went clear to the bottom. Pablo guessed this had to be close to 300 feet, before a new waterfall started. The figure was standing just next to the over-flowing water on the cliff edge, and suddenly slipped over the edge and swung over to the middle of the waterfall. With water blasting down on him from above, he slowly made the rappel down the cliff, centerline to the wall of water coming down upon him. Pablo could only imagine the weight of the water increasing the farther down he went. Suddenly he dropped out of sight at the base of the cliff.

The next canyoneer went over the edge in the same way. About halfway down, he started swinging from side to side like a pendulum at the base of a clock. He would go from one side, out of the waterfall, through and out the other, entirely disappearing in the water from time to time as he went. Pablo could hear, over the roar of the water, the hollering from the climber and the cheers from the remaining group at the top. This is crazy, he thought. One slip of that wet rope and he's a goner. But, one at a time, all made it down. The next two drop-offs were shorter but no less spectacular. Finally, at dusk, the group came in, wet, loaded down with climbing gear, dog tired, but still on a high from the day's adventure. To do both canyons back to back had never before been done. After much jubilation, the group decided it would be a good idea to get to bed. Clyde reminded them they had to get up, break camp, and get on the trail and up that wall all before the sun came up or most likely they wouldn't make it since it gets hot and there isn't one drop of water all the way up. No rebuttal came, and all crashed fast asleep within thirty minutes.

Pablo was awakened by horse bells coming into camp. Clyde was leading the first two in, and all the others followed. It was still pitch-black, but the animals seemed to be anxious to get out of this hot hole. Coffee was already made and Pablo helped himself. As they were saddling, Pablo looked across the valley and saw the group's headlamps bobbing about their campsite. They seemed to have taken Clyde's advice and were moving early. Soon, a trail of lights was seen leading out of their camp and up the trail, just as the last horse was saddled and the duo's camp load was secured. After leading the string over to the group's abandoned camp, Pablo and Clyde started loading all the gear. This went faster, since all the food and booze was gone and the loads were lighter. It was still dark when the loading was done and the duo started up the trail with Clyde in the lead.

After the first three switchbacks were completed, Clyde stopped and called to Pablo to unsnap the string. Pablo started from the back and met Clyde in the middle. Clyde then climbed back on his lead horse and with the first packhorse in tow started up the cliff trail. They were about one-third of the way up before the first morning glow. A pleasant breeze was still in the air and the temperature hadn't climbed yet. Great timing, Pablo thought. Up they went, back and forth, lunging and jumping up this almost 45-degree pitch with very few places to safely stop and rest the horses.

Pablo was amazed at the horses. No wonder Clyde only picks the A team for this type of trip. These animals are equal to any world-class Olympic athlete after years of training. Pablo just kept nudging his horse and holding on for dear life. Somehow, the horse string met the hiking group at the same time as all topped out at the rim. This gave time for a rest and for the snapping of the horses back to make a connected string. At this time Pablo walked over to the brass USGS benchmark stamped with JRH (Jesse Ray Hedgepath), squatted down, and kissed it, giving thanks he made it out alive again.

The climbers were wiped out. But given what they have been through, Pablo was surprised he didn't have to bring any of 'em out over a horse. That alone caused him to marvel at their toughness. To go down a canyon, on ropes, full of waterfalls, get back up, and do it again was a testament to the human spirit. When one trains well, is professional, and in top shape, one can push boundaries. A true professional never is a daredevil, but only one who takes calculated risks. Big difference. He would never again second-guess the power of Uncommon Courage.

CHAPTER 7

Bill

It was only 5:00 a.m., but after a two-day rest from the trip in and out of Tehipite twice, Pablo was rested and ready to go. He sauntered over to the corral, cup of hot fresh coffee in hand, where Clyde was already pulling out packhorses for the day's run.

Clyde spoke up first: "Well, Pablo, we're in for a relatively easy day today. Hauling gear only for a very nice family from Santa Barbara. Name's Kimbell. The husband and wife plus a few friends take this trip to the North Fork of the Kings River most every year. Only stay about four days and walk out on their own. You'll be surprised, Ann Kimbell is a real outdoorsy trooper. She's a small, cute gal who looks like she'd be your age, but the truth is that couple has four young children at home. I think this is the only getaway for them of the year, and they've earned it. On another note, we've got a new twist for today—and here he comes now."

Pablo looked up and saw a somewhat older man, fully dressed in cowboy gear, riding his horse up the road entrance to the station. He came to a complete strop near the duo, politely tipped his hat, and boldly announced, "WHAT A BEAUTIFUL MORNING." Pablo stepped back half a step, somewhat startled by the volume of the man's voice, but soon regained his composure.

Clyde spoke up, "Pablo, this is Bill. Bill, this is Pablo. Bill's gonna ride along with us today. Wants to get his horse legged up." Pablo remembered Clyde and Deb talking about Bill, a character who camps out over by the cow corral and helps the Clydes gather and rotate cattle all summer. Does the same during the winter down on the home ranch. Pablo had figured he was a somewhat antisocial type who mostly liked living alone, only venturing out into the human world on his own choosing.

Pablo, with his big inviting smile, announced, "Glad to meet ya, sir." Pablo was greeted back with a blank stare. "I'm not your daddy. Bill is good enough for me." Pablo turned to Clyde, who only lowered his hat brim while turning back to work. He then turned back to Bill and was met with a grin. Pablo relaxed and chimed in with, "Weather says there's a 20 percent chance of rain today. Got a raincoat, sir, or, I mean, Bill?" Bill looked down from his horse with his usual blank stare and replied, "Well, young man, that only also means there's an 80 percent chance it won't rain. And, as dried out as the country is this time of year, there's a 100% chance the rain won't do one bit of good. But, ya, I come prepared."

Bill rapidly dismounted, tied up his horse to the hitching rail, and went straight to the next packhorse to saddle 'em, knowing exactly what needed to be done. The group started to show up at the loading dock from their tent cabin and deposited their camping gear to be preloaded. Petite Ann came walking up with two large duffel bags hanging over her slender shoulders by the straps and lifted and dropped them on the dock. All Pablo could do was stare in frozen silence thinking, darn, Clyde was right.

Just about then he felt a sharp thump on his right shoulder where Clyde poked him, quietly saying, "Get your eyes back in your head and finish saddling." Pablo, startled back to reality, did just that. Bill noticed the Pablo show and chuckled to himself, thinking, "Yep, that boy has a long road of life ahead of 'em."

Soon, the hiking group was out the gate and on their way. Loading up five packhorses' worth of gear in the flatbed and then putting the total of eight horses in the trailer all went smoothly. All Clyde did then was look at the statue-still Dinkey, who was awaiting her command, point to the truck, and say two words: "Load up." In Dinkey went like a shot and quickly laid down to make herself as small as possible, hoping no one would change their mind and make her stay home. Stopping by the cookhouse, the trio received their lunches from Deb, as well as a "Have Fun" send off, and away they went out the gate.

As they rolled up the road toward the trailhead, Pablo thought a moment, and then asked, "Bill, I thought all cowboys had a dog. Where's yours?" Bill calmly replied, "Pablo, ya might as well ask me if I want a wife. Both of 'em need a lot of attention. Horses are enough for me. All ya got to do is feed 'em and they're happy. They don't ask to come in the house and bother ya. Just throw 'em a flake of hay and they're happy as all get out. Nope, don't need any more dependents than that. Yep, Pablo, you'll find in life there are some guys that would rather travel light. Not be shouldered with a heavy load, meaning wives, kids, dogs, big house mortgage, expensive car payments, need to keep up with the neighbors and all. A quiet, wide open place to set up my camp, have my couple of horses, and I'm perfectly happy. Having internet is one of God's greatest inventions. I can sit quietly out in the open spaces and keep up with all the world's events without having to live in it. Yep, gives one a different perspective viewing the world from arm's length. When I get tired of world events, I just turn off the laptop, go outside where all is quiet, and say hi to the squirrels, deer, and soaring hawks while petting my horses, reaffirming all is good."

Pablo quietly remembered something Clyde told him last year. "If everybody was the same, this world would be a boring place." He pondered this all the way up to the trailhead. After unloading the stock, the trio started loading the five packhorses with the guests' gear. Pablo and Bill lifted the loads and Clyde did the tarp and tying. They had this down pat and within thirty minutes were ready to be on their way. While Bill walked off into the woods for a quick nature call, Pablo asked Clyde about Bill's odd outlook on life.

Clyde smiled and responded, "Bill has earned the right to do and think anyway he wants. He served this country as a Marine in Vietnam and has seen all the ugly things humans can do to each other. I don't blame him for keeping society at a distance. The craziness just keeps on going, if ya pay attention to the news. But don't let that bother you. Keep on your own path and make your own way. Never stop observing and appreciating the small wonders of the world. That's what life is really about."

With Bill's return, the group was soon all mounted, Bill in the lead, Pablo second, pulling three packhorses, and Clyde following with the remaining two head. The morning sun was just cracking over the ridge, warming up the riders, and all was good.

After about thirty minutes up the trail, Pablo couldn't help noticing how Bill kept looking down to the side of his horse as if inspecting something in the trail. That got Pablo's attention, and he looked down and noticed a set of bare human footprints in the trail going their same direction. He thought that very strange up in this high country, with rocks, pine cones, and all the branches. Pablo finally spoke up to Bill, asking what's with the barefoot tracks. All the others have boots on. Bill just looked back and replied, "Nothin' surprises me anymore."

Clyde just smiled, since he had seen the friend of the Kimbell's back at the station without shoes and remembered him from past years. He was a member of a small group that believed shoes were an unnecessary habit of society and we would be better off without 'em, so our feet could toughen up as God intended. He had read a little about this group and discovered they were all young, and the guys all sported ponytails. He thought of it as another temporary focus of youth that, no doubt, would eventually pass. He saw no potential harm to others, so he simply shrugged his shoulders. Besides, Clyde figured this young man might feel a little bit protected since he knew a foot doctor was following him. Anyway, in the past the young gentleman always seemed to make it to the campsite. So, to each their own.

After about two and a half hours, the trio was approaching Post Corral Meadow. In the distance was the distinct sound of a helicopter. As the group approached the creek, crossing with the wide flat meadow on the other side, the helicopter came into view. It circled three times, getting lower each time. Clyde immediately instructed all to dismount and tie up for safety. There was a man and woman of senior age standing next to the creek and landing zone. Clyde walked up and asked if there was an emergency medical situation. Both just shook their heads no. They replied, "All of a sudden, our quiet moment was shattered with all this racket." With an inkling of what this was all about, Clyde walked back to his horse and retrieved his cell phone and two-way radio. Pablo could only look on with puzzlement. Bill gently jabbed him with his elbow to get his attention and muttered, "This is going to be interesting."

After the helicopter landed and the engine was shut down, Clyde walked up to the right side of the airship, where he could get a close-up view of the numbers on the side. He then calmly snapped a picture with his phone. He then proceeded to walk into the pilot's view and motioned for him to exit and have a discussion. He could see the one passenger looked like a biologist in a utility company uniform. She noticed Clyde and mysteriously stayed on the left side after exiting.

The pilot was evidently all proud of his flight in as he approached. Clyde calmly asked, "Do you have any search and rescue or any medical evacuation reason to get prior authorization from the US Forest Service to fly in here in the middle of the summer?" The smile quickly left the pilot's face. He replied, "The new utility company biologist wanted to get a survey of the snow site measurement locations and make sure there aren't any trees in the way. Here is her twelve-inch handsaw to take care of any problems."

Clyde just kept up the blank stare, waiting for any further response. With none coming, he proceeded. "Well, are you aware that the only flights authorized to come in below the 500 foot minimum elevation and land in a wilderness area are for medical emergencies or search and rescues? Not for a sightseeing trip by a new employee?" By then the young biologist was cautiously rounding the nose of the ship and approaching the duo. Clyde continued, "Well, young lady, do you have anything to add to this situation?" The pilot spoke up, saying, "I had no say in this. I was ordered by her and the utility to fly her in." Clyde thought, what a chump, throwing her under the bus.

"So, you didn't think you had any reason to notify Forest Service Dispatch of your flight plan when you left? There could have been a search, rescue, or even a fire going on, which require multiple aircraft in the area. And in you would come, blindly. That's why prior approval is necessary and why it's for emergencies only. Another thing, the whole concept of keeping unnecessary helicopter traffic out in the summer is to preserve the quiet wilderness experience these hikers and guests expect and deserve. You come flying in here like you own the place only because you are too darn lazy to hike in yourself. You'll have trouble explaining this to the FAA while you're begging 'em to let you keep your pilot's license. And you, young lady, your new employment with the utility company may be short lived. I hope you learn from this experience. My advice is to get back into that ship and leave the wilderness area immediately. Expect a grilling from both your bosses when you return. They'll know all about it before you even get landed."

Clyde turned and walked away, pulling the two-way radio out of his back pocket and calling for USFS Dispatch in the process. By the time Clyde was back to the horses, the two had jumped back into the helicopter and the engine was started. Within minutes, the helo lifted off and disappeared above the treetops and over the mountain, heading straight back down to the valley. Clyde looked to Bill and Pablo and explained, "Sometimes, especially with new employees, the utility company feels they are above the law and rules don't apply to them. So, checking them on the rules raises the awareness level so as to respect the solitude the wilderness users expect and deserve."

Clyde then turned to the elderly hikers, saying, "I hope now you can enjoy your well-deserved quiet wilderness. Have a nice trip." Turning back to Pablo and Bill, he said, "Let's mount up and hit the trail. I'd like to still beat the Kimbell group to their camp."

Pablo just stood still, mouth open and dumbfounded. Bill, with a grin, snapped his left shoulder with his index finger and said, "You heard the man." Pablo composed himself and slowly mounted and nudged his horse into a slow walk, still trying to digest all he had just encountered.

Within one hour the pack string encountered the Kimbells. They were all doing well, even Mr. Barefoot. After some small talk, mostly about the annoying noise from the helicopter, Bill turned his horse uptrail and gave it a slight amount of pressure with his heel. But Pablo sat still, just staring at Ann. Clyde, noticing this, said, "Pablo, time to get focused on work." This startled Pablo, who quickly composed himself and got his horses moving to catch up with Bill. Clyde rode past Ann and gave her a grin and tip of his hat. Ann responded with a smile and a wink. Both recognized a moment of the innocent infatuation of youth. It was obvious to Clyde she took it as a compliment.

As they continued along, Pablo's mind returned to the contents of their gear and the work ahead of unloading. He thought of the multiple cases of canned beer, knowing this was only a one-way dunnage service, and voiced his concern to Clyde. Clyde's response was, "Yea, they like to party. Can't blame 'em. Nice to get away from the kids, even if for only four days. But I can tell you, they smash down each and every can and backpack every one of them out themselves. In all the years they've been coming here, I never found even a trace of litter left behind. Ya, we pack in a lot of what some people would consider extra, but if they pack everything out, then no harm done. This group is definitely environmentally aware."

Bill just grinned and said, "I remember when I used to drink a lot. Gave it all up when I got divorced." Noticing the confused look on Pablo's face, he continued, "With the divorce, that eliminated the reason. Haven't had to touch a drop since. Sometimes life gives you a silver lining." Pablo just shook his head and blinked, thinking, that was a new twist on his prior assumptions. Bill continued, "No way am I interested in going back into bondage. However, I've been giving much thought to finally getting myself a dog. I know they are just another depen-dent, but at least when ya come home late, a dog will immediately forgive ya. A wife never will."

Clyde, who had been quietly smiling, finally spoke up. "Pablo, like I told ya last summer, your single, most important choice in life is who you choose for a spouse. You absolutely have to hit that one out of the park. Your spouse is your life partner and you have to get it right. Give yourself plenty of time before you decide. However, nowa-days, I see so many young folks take too long. Their clock is ticking, but by the time they decide they

BILL AND LULU

are are ready to take the next step, all the good ones are gone. Usually the ones that are left are still single for a reason. So the answer is to take your time, but not too much time. You're nineteen now. Because of your medical career goals, you've got a good ten years more of education. Best to get as much of that behind you as you can before your decision. That's only fair to your spouse. I'm glad I waited until all my education and training was done before I made the jump. Deb's been the best life partner anyone could ask for."

Pablo noticed Bill nodding in agreement. Then he said, "Yep, Clyde, you knocked that one out of the park."

As they descended down the mountain gorge toward the North Fork of the Kings river, the pack string went back and forth over the open granite slabs. Pablo was amazed how the horses never slipped on the glacier-polished surface, which was covered with decomposed granite that created the effect of literally walking on marbles over a smooth slate. Clyde called up to Pablo, saying, "These horses are raised from babies walking over this stuff and learn how to stay upright. The last thing they want to do is fall. And we riders are grateful for their learned skill."

Arriving at the predetermined campsite, Clyde knew the Kimbells usually went swimming first, then would come over and retrieve the camping gear. He wanted to get all unloaded as soon as possible and headed back up the trail. He knew if he didn't hustle, he would probably have to pry Pablo off the rock boulder with the perfect view of Ann diving in the water.

After tying up his horse, Pablo took a slow look around. This area of the North Fork of the Kings River, known as the Pot Holes, was truly a work of natural wonder. The swirling action of the river current over thousands of years with the small rocks and gravel has made the perfectly round pools just right for a midday dip. The water slows down to a calm, circular motion, so it takes minimal effort for one to stay in the center. The Kimbell group was starting to arrive and went straight to the nearest pool and jumped in. The midday sun reflecting off the rocks made it perfect for sun-drying

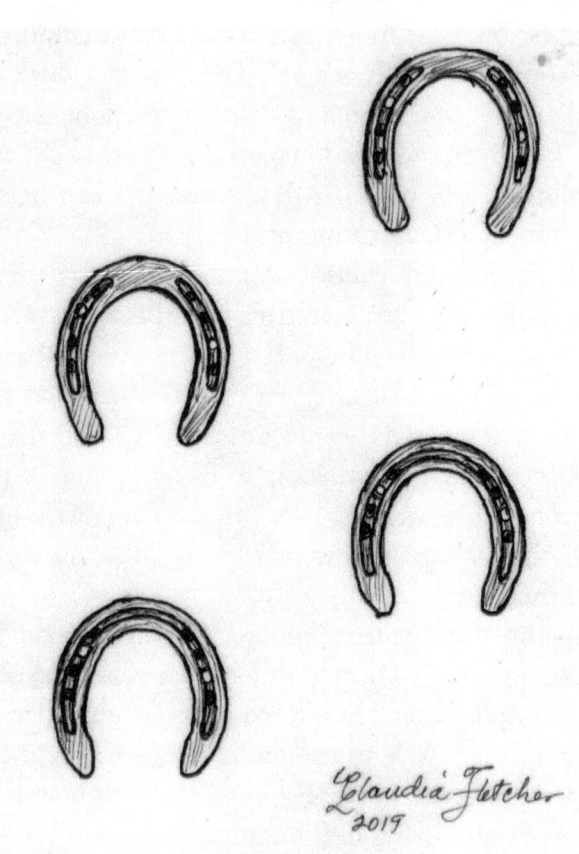

Horseshoes

after getting out. Only after quickly drying off and being rid of all the sweat and dust from the trail did they come over to camp and collect their gear. Even Mr. Barefoot didn't care if the rocks were hot. The first thing each one did was pop open a beer, sit under the shade of the nearest Jeffery pine, and enjoy their beverage. With the gentle upcanyon breeze, they proclaimed that this area is truly a magical example of nature's artistic ability. Clyde, Bill, and Pablo tipped their hats and bid them farewell.

As the trio ascended the mountain out of the river gorge, Pablo thought this was yet another day in paradise. On the way, Pablo noticed Bill fussing with his hat . . . taking it off, adjusting it, and placing it back on his head, then repeating the process. Finally Pablo had to ask him, "What's the problem with your hat?"

"Well, I have an odd-shaped head. That means when I finally get a hat broke in, it's usually worn out and it's time for another one to start over on. But that's OK. Just another cross to bear."

Popping over what's called the Overlook, the group came into a relatively flat area referred to by Forest Service botanists as a "flower pot." This is an area with multiple different tree species, including many lodgepole pines and red furs. A few right next to the trail were huge. Clyde stopped at the base of one of them and pointed up. "Pablo, follow this line seemingly carved out of the bark as it spirals up the trunk to about two-thirds the way to the top. It reminds you somewhat of a barber pole's single spiral strip. Well, that's from lightning. It hits toward the top and makes its way down to the bottom. When it meets the ground is where it blows out and sometimes starts a fire. Look around at the bases of the larger trees as your travel through an old forest area, especially along a ridge line as we are. Most of the time they just burn themselves out, but other times it can start a several-thousand-acre fire. That's been nature's way of intermittently cleaning the forest floor for thousands of years. For the last one hundred years, man has been putting out every little fire he comes across, and preventing nature from cleaning the forest floor. Results are this thick density of trees and brush. When a fire does get started, with the right hot, dry, and windy conditions, all this fuel on the forest floor leads to an explosion of flames that kills everything in its path. We can go on and on as to why this practice was used, but on an upcoming trip I will show you what serious devastation really looks like. It will shock you. But for now, just enjoy the ride and view."

Clyde didn't relax until the string was well past the flower pot and out of sight of the camp. Only then did Pablo's head get turned around straight so he could pay attention to where he was going.

Beyond the flower pot area the trail wound through a dense blueberry zone. Some of the berries were just getting ripe with good color, and evidence of bear activity was in the area. As the group approached a small meadow area off to the right of the trail, Bill suddenly pulled up on his horse and pointed. On the opposite edge of the meadow was a black bear lying under a lodgepole watching him back. Bill turned back in his saddle and quietly said, "He has an average size body but a large head. Can see some gray hairs on 'em too. Bet he's an old guy. Let's saunter over and get closer."

The whole group got to within twenty feet of the old bear. Pablo could see his calm eyes and the graying hair around the nose. He still had a full coat of jet-black fur with no worn or bare patches on his hide, and had huge feet with long claws. No sign of any cubs. Bill, being in the lead, calmly started speaking gently, "Well, old man, think ya can get through another winter? Bet you're not thinking about that one bit, are ya? You're all full with berries now and not in the mood to get up and challenge us, are ya? Yep, on this perfect day, life is good for you, isn't it? Well, you just relax and enjoy the rest of the afternoon. Hope to see ya again." After tipping his hat, Bill turned his horse to get back on the trail and all the other horses just followed in line without a single quiver. The horses did not feel threatened and thus stayed calm. It's all in the body language. Getting back on the trail, not a word was spoken for the next half-hour.

Soon the group was passing through Post Corral Meadow again. All was quiet. The senior couple was still relaxing in their camp and waved as the string filed by. Bill did the usual stopping of all the horses before the creek crossing to let any animal go pee before entering the water. Only two needed to go, so soon they were in the crossing and stopped to get a drink. Horses usually drink twice. They take a first drink, then they lift their heads to look around before dropping down again for a second long gulp. After this was done, the eight horses proceeded across the creek and back on the trail to continue the steady march.

It was about two o'clock by this time, and that's when the group started to meet hikers with their heavy backpacks heading into the wilderness from the trailhead. Pablo always liked these encounters. Slowing down slightly to keep the horses calm and steady gave him some extra moments to ask 'em where they're headed and where their home town is. Pablo enjoyed the responses he got. Most were eager to talk about hoped for destinations. There were always the usual questions about mosquitos, people, firewood, and how's the fishing. He loved the conversations, especially discovering that some came long distances to hike these trails, like from New York, Florida, and even a few from Europe.

A few clouds came over and the temperature dropped a little. The treetops were swaying and the sound of the wind was an ever-increasing backdrop symphony to Pablo's ears. The chipmunks seemed to scurry faster and the horses picked up the pace to get back to the trailhead. Bill seemed to know this and saw no need to touch his horse with his heels. Just let them pick their own pace.

Passing the turnoff to Hobbler Lake, the group started the descent toward Courtright Lake. Not far down the trail, the lake was visible through a narrow tree opening. Pablo only had a short time to view it because the opening was quickly closed by the dense tree canopy and the trail next went through some steep, rocky steps and switchbacks. Slowing the string down through this was essential. Much better to give each animal that extra needed step and get through slowly then to try and rush and have a serious wreck. Pablo knew, life in general went much smoother when you slowed down and paid attention through the more difficult portions. This allowed you to relax during the smooth-sailing sections. He used this method during school too. Many of his studies he could breeze through, but often he had to stay 100 percent focused in order to understand everything. That led to a much easier time down the learning path. At least, until the next treacherous part.

He was also developing an ear for the small sounds of trail riding. That of any horseshoes that might be getting loose. The hint of a horse's out of the ordinary, extra heavy breathing, or any signs of sweating on the horses. If so, he needed to slow down and sometimes stop and let 'em blow, if necessary. The last thing he would want is to overpush. This whole processes was a marathon, not a sprint. To go the distance, one needed to keep a steady pace and pay attention to details. He discovered the same was true in school as well as here. Soon he passed one of his favorite spots, the tiger lily pool. Most of the time the water was slow moving and not a great place to get a drink, and the trail was too close anyway. But just the sight of this small, creature-filled oasis just off his saddle stirrup always caught his eye and filled him with wonderment.

Another group of five hikers came by after getting an obvious late start. But no problem, there were plenty of places to camp for this eager group that just wanted to get on the trail after a long day of driving from LA. Pablo couldn't blame them. Any place in the wilderness is better than a blacktop parking lot.

After about twenty minutes, human chatter could be heard up ahead, coming toward them. Soon a group of excited high school hikers appeared. Their common backpacks tipped Pablo off that they were a group from Outward Bound. After small talk with these individuals, most of whom were only two to three years younger than himself, Pablo tipped his hat and said, "Adios, and buenas noches." Most knew what he was saying and returned his words with a wave and a big smile.

The time went by fast for Pablo. No sooner did he settle back into his saddle then the group was riding up to the trailhead and hitching rail. Unloading the packhorses went quickly since all the lash ropes were coiled, and the pack tarps were already folded and packed in the pack bags. Also, some of the bags were doubled inside each other, which allowed some of the packhorses to come out empty.

Right about then, Pablo heard a drop of rain hit his hat. Sticking out his hand, he felt another drop hit his palm. Looking up, he noticed Bill had a smile on his face.

"Well, Pablo," Bill said, "told ya we didn't need no raincoats. This little cloud will only amount to a six-inch rain. You know, a drop every six inches. Besides, when ya have your head right and with a good outlook, things usually work out to your liking. Now let's help Clyde get finished, load 'em up, and get pack to the station. Don't want to keep Deb waiting with dinner, now do we?"

Shoeing front foot tied up

CHAPTER 8

It Takes a Village

There were days where more than one trip was scheduled. When this occurred, one trip may be of moderate size and the other was only allowed if it was smaller. For example, two packhorses out on a one-day run, meaning in and out on the same working day. This was one of those days.

Deborah was taking two packhorse loads out to Post Corral Meadow, unloading, and returning. She was expected back around 3:00 p.m. at the latest, thus it was a relatively easy trip. No way was Clyde going to overload Deb on any solo run.

Deb's group consisted of a father, his wife, and their two young sons, about nine and eleven years of age. All were walking. The father had gone in a few days early and was planning to return back as far as Post Corral Meadow to meet his incoming family.

By 7:30 a.m., at the Courtright Spike station next to the Maxon Trailhead, Deb bid the trio, the mother (a family practice doctor) and her two sons, good hiking, and they started out. Deb loaded the gear and started following about forty-five minutes later. Within one and a half hours, Deb passed the trio. The two sons were doing well, but Mother was a little on the slow side, although saying she was getting her wind and was starting to feel better. Deb said good-bye and kept on her route.

As she passed the turnoff to Hobler Lake, her appreciation returned for the dedication of the ground-level USFS employees. There is a level one (lowest priority) trail which turns north here, going past Hobler lake and on up to the Snow Pillow weather station set up in Upper Burnt Corral, a meadow area overseen by the California Department of Water Resources (DWR). Like the one in Blackcap Basin, it's used to measure the water amounts of the Sierra snowpack. This information is critical to maintain flood control and agriculture management. This trail hadn't been cleared in over twenty years, and in many places was totally overgrown. The DWR needs to maintain this facility annually, yet the route was getting almost impassable. The DWR even offered to pay for the trail clearing, if the USFS didn't have the funds.

An attempt was made to set up this trip last fall, but the trail crew replied they were so totally exhausted they didn't want to even think of clearing out another tree that year. Totally understandable. So the project was bumped for a later year discussion. Just one month ago, during the Clydes' annual operating plan meeting in late spring, it was announced to the Clydes that the trail crew did indeed go back in and clear the entire route. They had saved that information to be a surprise at the spring meeting. And indeed it was. Somehow, they had mustered the energy to go back out again with winter coming on and knock this section out. There had been several short clearing trips, mainly using this route as a filler job to complete Forest Service personnel tours of duty. These crew members were Joe Ryan, Tyler Ross, Timothy Crosby, Jackson Fitzsimmons, Armando Puentes, Evan Tirey, and Ashley Edwards. Tracy Knapp was also out and working. She was the new Wilderness Manager for the Sierra National Forest, and it's been great to see someone who has a huge desk job get up and out in the field. Trail clearing isn't easy, being done with two-man handsaws called misery whips. Looking down at their hard trail work, Deb hoped these young individuals would maintain this work ethic and sense of responsibility as they proceeded in their USFS careers and in life. It upped her faith in the next generation.

Deb gently nudged her riding horse, Mesa, with her heel and again resumed her progress, leading the two packhorses. Proceeding on down the slope toward Long Meadow, in a thick stand of red and white fir trees, she came to a sudden stop. There, standing thirty feet directly in front of her on the trail, was a cinnamon bear, facing toward her. Both stood staring at each other. Fortunately the horses didn't seem to be getting nervous, yet even so Deb decided to just be patient and let things unfold. The bear then stood up on his hind legs and Deb noted they were then at equal eye level, with her sitting on the horse. She still stood her ground, even though the horses were now getting a little antsy. This pause lasted several seconds, until finally the bear dropped down to all fours, turned off the trail, and lumbered down the mountainside. Deb didn't proceed until the bear was well out of sight of the horses, as she knew there would be commotion enough when the horses smelled the scent when they came upon its spot on the trail.

That's exactly what happened. As she proceeded and crossed the bear's tracks, the horses snorted and started jumping sideways. The only thing to do was to keep at a steady pace forward and try to keep 'em on single file and on the trail until they calmed down. The last thing she wanted to happen was for the string to swing around and get in front of her. This could cause a major wreck and put her in serious harm's way, as the lead rope would wrap around her, which could be lethal. Sometimes it's necessary to pick up the pace just to keep the horses occupied, but it wasn't needed in this case. Soon all was calm again and Deb could relax and go back to enjoying the morning sun.

On down the hill she progressed, passing through Long Meadow, then back into the trees and down toward Post Corral Meadow. Crossing the creek, she meet the husband, and both sat down on a log next to the campsite and took a break. The horses stood statue still, as they were still full from their all-night grazing and had only been on the trail for about three hours. Small talk was exchanged, including discussion of his wife struggling somewhat. It appeared it would be a relatively late arrival for the trio.

With the gear unloaded and the pack bags repacked with the ropes and tarps, Deb was soon on her way back, after waving adios and encouragement to the husband to just relax and have fun.

No bears were seen on the journey back up through the trees, but when she got back to the Hobler Lake turnoff, she noticed the two boys sitting beside the trail, no mom in sight. The youngest of the boys said he had left his mom back down near the bottom of the steep grade of the hill, sitting on a rock. She had told him to go up and join his brother, which he dutifully did.

The boys had been sitting there for over two hours and Deb had a bad feeling. Since it was getting to be late afternoon, she instructed the older boy to head on up the trail and inform dad about the situation and have him come back here. She then told the younger son to follow her back down the trail to find Mom. The more Deb progressed down the trail, the more worried she became. But she finally reached the mother, who was sitting on a rock over ten feet off the trail, clear down at the base of the grade, not much farther that when where she had passed her on the way in. This poor woman had an expressionless face and a glazed look in her eyes. Deb knew she was in trouble.

The young son was stunned to see his mom in this condition and stood still on the trail, as per Deb's quiet instructions. Deb dismounted and slowly walked up to the woman, not wanting to startle her. When Mom turned around, she jumped up and started to run into the forest. Deb started talking gently and managed to get her stopped after only a few running steps. After slowly approaching, the mom maintained her blank stare as Deb asked her what her name was. She only slowly shook her head. Then, gently, Deb examined her head, neck, and back to determine if she had fallen and sustained any trauma. This was all negative. The remaining extremity exam also proved normal.

Deb asked the young son if he knew if his mom was taking any medications, and he only shrugged his shoulders and said, "I don't think so." Her water bottle was still half full, so Deb knew it had been filled to the top at the start of the trip, and it hadn't been hot that day. Her pulse and breathing were normal. So, most likely, dehydration was not at play, just severe exhaustion and confusion. As the mother's composure started to return with Deb's gentleness, she was able to take some steps back up onto the trail with her arm around Deb's shoulder.

Getting back to the trail was one thing, getting *up* the trail to Post Corral was an entirely different matter. Therefore, the only way forward was for Mom to ride Deb's horse. So, after climbing up on a rock with Mesa calmly positioned next to her, Mom was able to be lifted up and into the saddle with the help of Deb and the son. She seemed stable enough with both hands on the saddle horn. Mom began to remember people's names, and then recall how she had gotten totally disoriented and confused during her hike and couldn't remember much until now. Deb felt the mom's mental state was recovering, so she took the lead rope and started walking back up the trail, leading Mom on her horse and the empty packhorses, and followed by the son. Deb had to keep a close eye on Mom's composure, but she felt confident it was improving and that the decision to keep going was a sound one. The last thing she wanted was for Mom to pass out, fall off the saddle, and get injured.

As the group topped the trail's climb at the turnoff to Hobbler Lake where Deb had met the two sons, no dad had arrived yet. The sun was getting low on the mountain ridge top, so going forward was the only option, since all the camping equipment was at Post Corral.

Mom was getting more and more talkative by the time the group got to Long Meadow. It was in this area that they started hearing voices, most surely from Dad and the older son. As they came into view, Mom perked up even more. The reunion of the family members was heartwarming, but the sun was getting lower and Deb urged they best stay on the move. Keeping the rider in the saddle, Deb picked up the pace a little. This went on for another one and a half hours until they reached camp at Post Corral Meadow.

After Dr. Mom got off the horse and back down to reality on the ground, she broke down and cried uncontrollably. It had dawned on her that she had not been able to make rational decisions, and could easily have wondered farther off the trail if Deb had not located her in time. She might not have been found for days, and that's how people in her situation die. In her altered state mind, she could easily have walked of a rock cliff.

After seeing that Mom was on her way to full recovery, Deb remounted and headed back home again. She didn't get to the trailhead until well after dark, which she knew would be worrying Clyde. The first thing she did was get in the truck radio and check in with a brief explanation for her delay. After unsaddling the horses and loading 'em up, she finally was able to head out the gate and toward home.

About two months later, Deb received a heartfelt letter from the mom. She hadn't realized how bad of shape she was in until Deb came upon her and helped get her orientation back. In retrospect, she knew she was in trouble, and if left alone to wonder off-trail in the dark, in an altered mental state, her chances of survival would have been greatly compromised. She sincerely wanted to thank Deb for most likely saving her life.

This is brought up to make a point. It doesn't matter what your educational background is, if you go into the wilderness, whether for a day hike or a two-week trek, STAY TOGETHER. By not observing that hard but simple rule, those boys could have easily lost their mother.

The next day, Deb got to stay in and rest and Pablo and Clyde went out. This was for a group of hikers to Blue Canyon, in Kings Canyon National Park. There happened to have been a lightning strike fire in the area. The USFS was following a "let burn" policy on this occasion, and there was an onsite fire crew as well as daily overflights. The Blue Canyon area was east of Crown Valley and up to Kettle Ridge, which is the start of the park.

The group seemed to be well-experienced hikers, and after explaining the situation with the fire, they all opted to proceed with the trip. They knew full well they would be going near the fire line, and might need to make a wide detour or even abort the whole trip if the fire got out of hand. Clyde had been well-versed on the fire by the USFS, and they had given him the green light. He advised the group the trail past Crown Valley was the actual fire line, or defense zone, so they would have to be careful or may even be ordered to go around. Nonetheless, at daybreak the hikers departed the trailhead, fully informed. It was an eight-hour horse ride to Blue Canyon, and for hikers to make it in one day is truly a heroic effort. The trail is relatively level until Crown Valley, then soon after it starts to go up about 1,000 feet over Kettle Ridge, then give all that elevation away as it goes down the back side and up to Blue Canyon itself.

Shortly after passing Crown Valley, Pablo and Clyde encountered the fire crews. They had used the trail as their fire line and had started the backfires all along the north side for about half a mile. The fires were started early in the morning and were burning comfortably far away from the trail. The fire was about 400 acres total, and in the slow cook stage. Perfect to clean up the forest floor as nature intended. The on-the-ground fire crew gave the go-ahead to Pablo, Clyde, and the hikers to proceed with caution.

Pablo was amazed, while going down the trail, at the difference that could be seen already on either side of the trail. On his right was the usual thick tangle of downed small, dead trees intermingled with the dense overgrown thickness of new trees, all trying to compete for the same sunlight, water, and ground nutrients. On his left, even though it was still smoking, the forest floor was noticeably cleaner. With the right wind direction, he could see sunlight getting to the forest floor, whereas none was getting through on his right. All the small new trees were burned, leaving the older large trees with some burn scarring, but still standing tall, and with green tops. He realized that the landscape being created on his left would grow into the same as what the California Native Americans lived in for 10,000 to 15,000 years. He knew by his reading that the California Natives would set fires on purpose. However, these were usually only five- to twenty-acre fires meant to make small clearings for better hunting. The larger fires, those set by lightning, were another matter. These they had no control over. Think about it: they didn't have access to airplanes or bulldozers to fight big fires. They simply moved their camps out of the way, let nature take its course, and moved in again the next year. With this approach, the forest of the past was healthier in many ways and life moved on.

Fortunately, the wind kept moving from south to north, keeping the sky clear of smoke. After passing this area, they started climbing Kettle Ridge. At the top a great view was obtained by looking back and seeing the whole fire progress through the 400 acres, doing nature's cleaning.

Topping over, they started to lose altitude again. The sound of Blue Canyon Creek was getting louder as they went until soon they were traveling up the canyon next to its banks. Pablo and Clyde had already passed the hikers by then, but Pablo knew they were all heading in the right direction. Finally popping into view was Blue Canyon Valley itself, a welcome sight for Pablo. He hadn't been there since last summer, and it was even more beautiful than he remembered. With its tall green grass, high granite walls on both sides, and a postcard-quality deep creek running though the middle, he had almost forgotten there were still beautiful places like this in the world. Yep, eons of time, let alone a single year, had not changed this place one bit—especially since it only gets about a dozen people passing through each year.

The route coming up via the creek was thick with dead and downed old tree growth and could use a lightning fire. Up here in the valley itself, they were near the tree line and the forest was naturally thin. Any fire started here wouldn't get far. Pablo could see evidence of that all around him. There were the occasional large, dead tree snags with burned-out bases. Obvious lightning strikes that didn't progress much past the base of the tree due to lack of fuel.

That evening was most relaxing for Pablo. With the narrow entrance to the valley at the south end, the whole area was a natural boxed-in enclosure for the horses. They had no desire to wander since all they needed was there. The soft ring of the horses' bells was soothing to him. Even though he had been here once before, he realized there was always more to observe and learn. Not only could he renew his appreciation for the surrounding natural beauty, he could more deeply realize the natural dynamics it takes to keep it that way.

The hiking group arrived before dark and, after diving into their gear, were all soon tucked into their bags and sound asleep. Pablo thought, "Ya, another end to a perfect day." Way upcanyon, far from the hikers' camp, Pablo suddenly noticed a head lamp bopping along the creek edge. He surmised the hiker group must have company. Oh well, plenty of room.

The next morning, Clyde was up at 5 a.m. getting coffee going. Pablo grabbed a cup, along with all the lead ropes, and set out to retrieve the horses from their night of grazing and resting. He found them in their usual stance a short distance away. Clyde always said, if they have had a good night, by morning they'll be standing around in a group, burping and talking politics. This morning was no different. Soon he had all the hobbles off and the horses strung together and headed back to camp. Even being in no hurry and enjoying the scenery, they still had all horses saddled and loaded by 7:30 and were heading down the trail.

Being in a deep, narrow canyon this early meant the sun didn't come up until well

Horse hobble on neck

into midmorning. Only then did it warm up enough so Pablo could take off his jacket. With the loud rushing creek on his left and the almost sheer cliff on his right, he realized this was the only route the trail could be on.

Clyde had told him about Blue Canyon at one time being a perfect location for a cattlemen family named Sample to place all of their replacement heifers for the summer. These are animals they didn't want to breed yet with the bulls, and thus had to be kept separated from any bulls until they were a little older. If they were allowed to breed too early, their pelvis wouldn't be developed enough to give birth, which would result in a stuck calf. In humans, this condition is called dystocia, and can be managed. But for cattle, it's usually fatal for both the calf and the young mother. Pablo knew that sometimes, if found in time, the calf can be pulled out manually and possibly saved, along with its mother, if you're lucky. In humans, this problem is addressed with a Caesarean section. In the open range where the cattle are mostly hidden from view, that procedure is generally not an option. It's just makes more sense to allow the young future mother time to reach proper maturity. Generally speaking, nature will take good care of her.

Being boxed in here was perfect for young heifers. They couldn't get out and the bulls couldn't reach them. With only a four-foot opening at the lower entrance and a three-pole removable gate to close it off after passing, it served its purpose perfectly. The small log cabin that housed the range rider was located just inside the gate, so a watchful eye could be kept with minimal effort. All until this whole area was subsumed in the expansion of Kings Canyon National Park. The cattle operation was forced to leave. The small cabin was now reduced to a no more than one-foot high pile of decomposing logs. One of the three gate poles was still visible, but it too would soon be returned to nature. Pablo had no doubt this area was used routinely by the Native Californians, since he always saw plenty of deer, quail, grouse, and fish whenever they rode through.

Pablo was in the lead pulling three empty packhorses, followed by Clyde pulling the one horse loaded with their camp equipment and the remaining two empty packhorses. Looking up and off to his left across the canyon, he stopped his string and pointed to a mother bear with two cubs grubbing in the hillside meadow. Just another morning for this young family, who didn't care at all about Pablo and Clyde with their horse string. There was a good chance they hadn't heard them because of the loud creek. Just the same, "keep moving and don't disturb" was usually the best option. The horses never gave 'em a second look.

As they started climbing up the canyon sidehill, Pablo could get more of a view of Tehipite Canyon. It's so much nicer up here than down in that hot hole, he thought. He totally understood why Clyde would try to talk people out of going down to Tehipite and instead consider these higher alpine areas. But, to each their own, Clyde always said. Everyone is entitled to one learning lesson.

Up and over the top they went. Heading back down the west side of Kettle Ridge was much easier. Going downhill, with the horses empty and all heading toward home, meant the animals were mostly on autopilot. Pablo's main job now was to simply enjoy the scenery. After crossing Crown Creek and passing Crown Valley, the well-used trail at this point was wide and open. The horse string was moving at a relatively fast walk, just eating up mileage. Coming around a blind bend in the trail, they all came to a sudden stop.

Just to the right of the trail, sitting on a rock, was a young man, still with his backpack on. He looked thoroughly wiped out, but had a firm, determined look on his face. Pablo and Clyde both stopped, and all just looked at each other for a silent moment, until Clyde finally broke the ice with, "Where'd you come from today, son?"

The young man slowly turned his head, neck, and shoulders, as if every move pained him, and replied, "Blue Canyon." Clyde replied with, "This morning?" "Yep," was the young man's reply.

Pablo then spoke up, saying, "Was that your head lamp I saw at the upper end of the canyon meadow late last night?"

"Yeah, I got in late last night and was looking for a place to bed down in the dark."

Pablo responded, "I didn't see you come by our camp via the trail."

"No, you didn't, because I came down the back way over the cliffs. Tough as hell, but I made it".

"There's brush that reaches way over your head on that route," said Clyde. "That was no picnic."

"I found that out the hard way. It's the reason I got to the bottom so late. But, I made it."

"We didn't see you on the trail until now," Pablo interjected. "How did you get past us?"

"I didn't realize this trail was here, so I just went downcanyon some and headed back over the cliffs in the least brushy place I could find. Mostly on my hands and knees until I got to the top. Started out at 4:00 a.m."

Clyde asked if he was trying to get all the way out today, to which the young man nodded and said, "Yep, have too."

"Well, young man," said Clyde, "you look pretty tired. This here is Pablo and I'm Clyde, the owner of the horsepacking operation in this part of the Sierras. We don't have an extra saddle horse but we do have empty packhorses. If you would like, I can carry your backpack out and meet ya at the trailhead or the station with it. That should help you out some."

The young man gave a long sigh before replying, "That's mighty kind, sir, but no thanks. I've come this far and would like to finish out on my own. But thanks."

"Sure enough, son, I see your point. Good luck to ya." Clyde tipped his hat while gently nudging his riding horse with his heel to get the string moving, and he and Pablo proceeded on down the trail.

Both rode for about fifteen minutes until Clyde broke the silence. "Pablo, that young man wasn't much older than you are. I have to admit, he sure has grit. Most young folks in this day and age wouldn't even think of such an off-trail trip, let alone actually tough one out. Yep, in your generation, those few like yourself and him, those who are willing to not listen to their peers, are able to break out and try a different path. And in addition, encounter problems, figure out solutions, and just tough it out. You may not realize it, but even though he may be a couple of years older than you, you're both of the same mindset. I can't say the same for the rest of your generation. Most just want to take the easy way out. But, you can look at it this way: both of you have a good chance of succeeding in this world in a big way. The reason is simple: your competition is so lame. Yep, you, Pablo, and that young man on the trail have a lot in common. You are both shining lights of your generation, in my view."

Clyde's words hit Pablo hard. He had never given it much thought. He had broken away from his generation's peer pressure over a year ago. It seemed now like a distant memory. He was proud of his accomplishments in college, in the saddle, and in his life's journey in general. He felt his attitude toward whatever the world threw at him was, "Bring it on." Now that Clyde had articulated it, he realized how different he was from most of his peers.

The duo continued their journey out to the trailhead uneventfully. They leisurely unloaded the packhorse and then led all the horses, one at a time, into their lineup in the trailer. Time to head home.

The slow drive was quiet. Pablo was silently enjoying the view, deep in thought on the day's events. Before they got to Wishon Dam, they came upon a lone hiker moving along slowly with a slight limp on the right side of the road. As they got closer, Clyde slowed down and said, "Recognize 'em?"

Slowly approaching the hiker, Pablo rolled down his passenger-side window while Clyde came to a stop beside the young man.

"Why don't you put your backpack in the truck," said Clyde, "and hop in and we'll give ya a ride to the station. There's only one road out and you have to go by us anyway."

He simply nodded his head in agreement and climbed in the back seat of the four door flatbed truck.

As they resumed their travel, Pablo asked, "How did you get by us again?"

"Well," he replied slowly in a Southern drawl, "guess I bypassed you all when I decided to cut across country and come out at a different trailhead."

"Where's your car?" asked Pablo.

"Don't have one. Hitchhiked up here from the airport."

"Airport!" Pablo responded in surprise while turning in his seat.

"Yep," he replied. "Flew out here from Alabama."

Pablo was silent. The only signal he got was a wink from Clyde before they turned into the station driveway.

After introductions to Deb were made, the young man was invited into the cookhouse while Pablo and Clyde took care of the animals. Deb insisted he eat dinner with them. No way was she going to turn him out.

During dinner it was discovered he was going to be a senior this fall at the University of Alabama and was a 4.0 student. He had been looking at maps of the Sierra Nevada Mountain Range in California and had planned out his trip and route after several months' consideration. He proclaimed he should get started back on the road, since he had to make it to the airport in Fresno to catch a 9:00 a.m. flight the next day. School was going to start soon.

Deb stepped in and said, "That's silly. I have a better idea. Why don't you go take a shower, put on clean cloths, wash your dirties, and get a good night's rest in the bunkhouse? There's an extra bed in Pablo's room. I'll give you a ride down the hill to the airport in the morning in time for you to catch your flight."

His mouth dropped. "You'd do that?"

"Of course I would. You have a mother somewhere and I'm sure she would appreciate it too."

That night, Pablo didn't get much conversation out of the young gentleman. After a few softly grunted answers to his questions,

Pablo could hear the slow, steady breathing of deep sleep. He was clearly exhausted.

The next morning, after a 6:00 a.m. breakfast, Deb and the young man headed out the gate in plenty of time to make the flight.

Pablo had finished putting the saddled horses in the trailer and he and Clyde were heading out for the day's trip. He still had on his mind the young gentleman from Alabama. He had felt he had met someone he could identify with as a fellow traveler on a common path of life. He felt enriched by the experience and knew he would never forget him.

During dinner that evening, Clyde asked Deb how it went at the airport. She said, "Well, we made it in time. He had told me he had a layover in Denver. So I asked him if he had any money for lunch and he replied, 'No, ma'am, not a cent.' So I gave him $20. He was shocked and gave me a heartfelt hug. I asked for his mother's phone number. Told him I'd tell her that he got on the plane and was heading home. Some things only mothers understand. His mother was most grateful and thanked me profusely. I told her she was more than welcome and ended with, 'It takes a village.'"

CORN LILY

Claudia Fletcher
2020

CHAPTER 9

The ID Team

About the middle of the summer season, much discussion was heard by Pablo of a special trip coming up. It seems the US Forest Service was going around talking to all the pack stations and doing an onsite inventory of all the trails they were using to judge for environmental impact. These included trails for the general public and any special pack station routes, called "user trails." These were trails off the main system routes. For some reason, it was felt all the pack stations operations had to be examined and their routes evaluated to determine if any adverse environmental issues were occurring—even though these operations had been conducted on the same trails for over eighty years.

Earlier in the summer, these Forest Service Identification Teams (or ID Teams, as they were called) had started systematically visiting all the pack stations in the Sierra National Forest part of the John Muir Wilderness. These teams would go out on their own for about ten days and do their work based on prior discussion with the individual pack stations.

Clyde had made the proposal of voluntarily providing pack support for the operation, bringing along a cook and supplying all the food. Initially, this was met with some skepticism by the USFS, and Pablo couldn't imagine why.

Clyde explained, "This group is made up of various environmental specialists, each an expert in their field. Historically, most have not been trusting of commercial outfitters' environmental sensitivities, and didn't feel their input was of any value. They felt the packers would adversely try to influence their pure, worthy cause. On the other hand, many, if not all, of them have no doubt

had been looked down upon by commercial outfitters and judged as trail-mix-eating tree huggers who wouldn't be caught dead having anything to do with pack stock in a wilderness area. Well, I feel it is high time to break the rut both groups seem to be in. I feel it's best to get together for several days over campfires and voice concerns and find some common ground. It worked for John Muir and President Theodore Roosevelt, so it should work for us."

The green light was given to Clyde's plan, and the start day was fast approaching. Pablo was getting the feeling this was going to be a trip he would never forget. He overheard Clyde talking on the phone numerous times with a gentleman named Dr. Calvin Wise. He was a pediatric dentist who had been in practice for several decades and was taking more and more time off to pack into the John Muir Wilderness. The reason Clyde wanted him involved was his remarkable ability as a camp chef, a key component to Clyde's plan to smooth things over with the USFS. But Pablo soon was to find that Calvin Wise was far more than a simple cook.

The day prior to departure, Dr. Wise arrived with his pickup packed full of kitchen equipment, food, and his own special camp gear—including, tucked under his left arm, a small Jack Russell

Terrier, whom he named simply "Dog." Pablo, seeing the dog's short little legs and knowing it could never keep up for the planned ten-day trip, thought this was going to be a major problem. He knew Clyde would never allow the dog to be carried by any of his horses. But Pablo's concern was lifted when Dr. Wise asked him to help him get his own horse out of the single-horse trailer he was towing. Out came the horse, and Dr. Wise calmly placed Dog on the horse's back, no saddle, and calmly led it to the holding pen.

As Pablo unloaded the pickup's gear and spread it over the width of the loading dock, he realized this wasn't going to be the usual pack trip. This was looking more like a campaign-type trip. All the food was stored in bear-resistant containers. The containers' front doors were locked, and when opened, revealed numerous drawers and cabinets. In addition, attached legs could elevate the boxes to a comfortable standing height. All was compact, neat, and complete. There were four of these containers, and it looked as if a whole commercial restaurant kitchen had been packed up and laid out before him. Dr. Wise also brought numerous individual, rolled up tables with legs to be attached, as well as tablecloth material, plus a good dozen individual folding camp chairs. Additionally, there was a twenty-by-thirty-foot plastic tarp to serve as a complete roof over the camp. And all this was only for starters. Pablo was dumbfounded. He had never seen such impressive gear.

Pablo started to realize how big the group was. There were eight people in the ID Team, each having a heavy backpack, and then the four of them—Deb, Calvin, Clyde, and himself—who alone would require six packhorses.

Since the ID Team wasn't to arrive until the next morning, it was time to get to work preloading the camp kitchen equipment and food supplies. This took most of the afternoon. Careful attention was taken by Dr. Wise as he looked over each day's menu and double-checked all the food, spices, cooking utensils, and so on. He was clearly a man who paid attention to detail. He had a stack of index cards listing each day's breakfast, lunch, and dinner.

Pablo noticed a large roll of drip line plastic tubing and asked what it was for. Calvin replied, "That, my fine young man, is something you will never stop thanking me for. It's for a water line from the nearest creek that will run into camp. Since I consulted extensively with Clyde as to the location of each night's campsite, I know how far away the nearest water source will be. By laying out this temporary line, we can get fresh water into the campsite continuously. That is why you won't have to be carrying water buckets all day. See, ya put a little garden screen hose end on the intake side to keep out wood debris and the magic happens."

The four kitchen boxes had their own pack straps for the saddles. So, with all else preloaded, the total load was to fill six more packhorses. That would be twelve in all. With their four riding horses, since the specialists were all walking, the total horse string was to be sixteen. Clyde advised, "Even though the USFS specialists all seem to be purists, we're going to bring along an extra saddle horse as an emergency taxi, just in case. Bet you a quarter he gets used."

With camp to be packed up and moved each day, Pablo realized how much he was going to be needed on this trip. Each day, for the whole trip, all seventeen horses would have to be saddled and loaded, led to the next campsite, and then unloaded and unsaddled. Each day's camp was about a four- to five-hour ride. This provided enough time for Calvin, Deb, Clyde, and him to unload and set up camp and make sure dinner was started. The specialists were to walk, stopping to work along the way, so timing had to be right for them to arrive at the next camp and have dinner waiting at 5:00 p.m. Clyde had told him, "We're going to start from Courtright Lake and make a big loop and come out at Wishon lake." Pablo got dizzy with just the thought.

The next morning came with predictable Clyde's movement in the corral at 5:00 a.m. The door was cracked open as the signal for Pablo to get started. He could hear Deb and Calvin talking in the next building and knew they were way ahead of him. Clyde was retrieving horses five and six by the time Pablo arrived and began his saddling work. Bill came by to help with the loading. He was to stay behind on the trip to shuttle the trucks with trailers over to the Wishon Lake exit point. The USFS vehicles were being moved by USFS personnel.

When all seventeen horses were caught and saddled, the duo took a break and went into the cookhouse for breakfast. Since the flatbeds had already been loaded with gear the night before, all that was left to do was load the horses. Just as the breakfast dishes were finished being cleaned and put away by Pablo and Clyde, all eight USFS specialists showed up. Pablo and Clyde quickly loaded all the horses in the two trailers, Dinkey jumped into the back of Deb's truck, and the caravan headed to the Courtright trailhead.

Upon arriving, the specialists unloaded their backpacks on the loading dock and Clyde introduced all to each other. After the formal introductions were done, the group headed out for the day's work after an agreed upon campsite for the night was established. With them gone, the four looked at the pile of work to be done. The silence was broken by Clyde saying, "Well, this stuff isn't going to load itself, so let's get at it."

An hour and a half later, all twelve packhorses were loaded and strung out, and the group was ready to head off. Deb, who was in the lead with Dinkey at her side, was pulling four packhorses. Pablo was next, pulling another four, and Clyde followed with the remaining four plus the empty saddle horse tied on behind. Dr. Wise was in the back with his ever-faithful Dog under his left arm. The "Let's go" signal was given and down the trail the campaign began.

It was quite a procession. With that many animals, Clyde dropped back about a quarter mile to split up the outfit. This minimized the potential interference with any hiking groups they might encounter. It was just a courteous gesture, but much appreciated due to the dust. Deb, in the front, had her radio on and would call back if she encountered any hiking groups. Good communication allowed for smoother travel.

The first night's camp was preselected to be at Burnt Corral Meadow. This was a four-and-a-half-hour ride, and the party arrived about 1:00 in the afternoon, giving them plenty of time to unload the gear, set up the kitchen for Calvin, and unsaddle all the horses and turn 'em out with hobbles. Every fourth horse was fitted with a bell to make it easier to locate them the next morning.

Upon returning to camp after his horse duty, Pablo got his first sight of what this caravan-type camp setup really looked like. The four kitchen boxes, now standing on their legs, were arranged in a semicircle fashion, with an elevated chef's worktable in the center. Also elevated on long legs was a three-burner propane stove. Right near the cook's station, a water line was pouring out into a five-gallon bucket some of the clearest, coldest water Pablo had ever tasted. This was from the line that marched slightly uphill to intercept the creek over 150 feet away. A pit, some ten feet across, had been dug and in it a roaring campfire was ablaze. Above that the twenty-by-thirty-foot heavy plastic tarp was spread. The tarp roof was supported by one of the sixty-foot ropes strung between two trees, and was also secured on all four corners and in the middle to keep the sides about five to six feet above ground. This raised the roof and allowed over ten feet of headspace in the center. The tarp covered the entire kitchen area, dining area, and campfire.

Pablo was amazed the leaping flames of the fire didn't burn a hole in the overhead tarp. The tarp seemed to simply lift itself up, and no harm was done. Calvin saw Pablo's look of wonderment and stated, "That's the phenomenon of heat rising. It lifts the tarp out of the way and the flames never get a chance to do any damage. You'll notice how warm it is under here. You can imagine how much heat is lost if it's not trapped and pushed back down. It stays quite cozy under here, even in cold pouring rain." Several days later, the weather was going to provide just such a demonstration.

Around 5:00 p.m., the eight-member USFS crew arrived at camp. Pablo could tell they were whipped. Usually, the first day out on a trip like this is a butt kicker, and their first day was no exception. They immediately went to work setting up their tents and sleeping bags and getting set for the night. In less than an hour, they started drifting into the covered camp area. It was starting to get chilly, and all were amazed as to how comfortable it was under the expansive tarp near the fire. There was plenty of room for all. No mention of what was on the menu was uttered, but Pablo observed how nobody hesitated to grab a seat at any table. When Calvin displayed the dinner, the USFS crew was shocked. Opening the lids to various pots, he showcased beef bourguignon (a Julia Child recipe), green salads, hot fresh-baked bread, and delicious peach flambé for dessert. The hearty cheers from the famished crew brought a grin to Calvin's face, and after that not a word could be heard for some minutes. All were totally focused on their dinner. Pablo saw Clyde give Calvin a wink followed by a thumbs up. Soon thereafter, the whole group joined in for a toast to Calvin.

With their bellies full, the whole dog-tired group began to turn in for the night. By 8:00, after the dishes were done and stowed, not a peep could be heard. Pablo lay in his small tent, listening to the nearby creek, and to the horses' bells calmly chiming as they lazily fed on belly deep grass. He couldn't believe how peaceful his whole world was.

Dr. Wise was up at his usual 5:00 a.m., getting coffee going and starting breakfast. The crew started showing up about an hour later. Over coffee they got together and composed their reports from their notes on the prior day's work. Noted was the pathetic condition the trail was in. This was due to it being downgraded to a lower maintenance priority because of tight budgets. No one could figure out how Clyde and crew were going to get all those packhorses around the deadfalls with no mishaps.

With all this duly noted, breakfast—a mountain of pancakes, plenty of syrup, and fried bacon—was served. When all were done eating, Calvin handed each of 'em a sack lunch and a "have fun today" smile. The work group packed away their respective small camps so they could be loaded on the horses, and soon were off for the day's work assignment. The evening before, Clyde had helped them outline numerous side routes on a map that the study group planned to evaluate. At the end of the day, all would rendezvous at the predetermined place and time to camp.

With the camp now relatively quiet, the four members of the packing crew sat down for a comfortable breakfast and that extra cup of coffee. Then Clyde and Pablo went out to collect the horses while Deb elected to stay and help Calvin arrange the kitchen to be loaded again.

As they walked up to the group of horses, carrying the lead ropes, Clyde stopped and told Pablo, "Look at those horses, bellies full, all watered up, lazily standing around swishing mosquitos off of each other's backs with their tails. I know they're just talking politics, so time to put 'em to work. You get the ones on the far left and I'll collect those on the right and we'll work toward the center. If they know they're being gently confined with each other as a group, it calms 'em down and nobody gets excited."

The duo removed the hobbles and secured each horse to the next. This was done by starting with a lead rope end looped around the front horse's neck and tied with a bowline knot, then next secured to the hair end of the tail, with the hair acting as part of the knot. This kept the rope from dropping down too low and getting tangled in the horse's rear legs. The tension was anchored on the neck, so at no time was any tension on the tail. The whole string was put together in this fashion and soon two lines of horses, eight in one and nine in the other, were quietly marched into the camp area.

After saddling all seventeen head, the camp was mostly pre-packed and ready to load. All four teamed up to load the pack-horses, which took a little over one hour. The one lonely saddle horse, named Camp, was going to get some company. The archae-ologist member of the USFS team was still wiped out from the day before and welcomed the taxi ride. On she went and the whole string started the steady march to the next camp.

They took a different trail system route to intercept the main trail artery, and then proceeded up to Red Mountain Basin. The next camp would be established at a most beautiful location near

Fleming Creek. This site provided a commanding view of the John Muir Wilderness's 11,000-foot eastern border and of the start of nearby King Canyon National Park. The trail would eventually lead over Hell for Sure Pass, which was quite properly named, as Clyde had pointed out to the group that the trail over the pass wasn't passable by stock anymore. No problem; the campsite was properly located to allow for the survey crew to head off in numerous directions. The time needed to get this area's work done would take all of two days, and being able to keep camp in one location for two consecutive nights was a welcome thought.

Arriving at the campsite, with the horses unloaded, hobbled, and set out to free graze, all attention focused on setting up camp and getting comfortable. Pablo could tell Deb was enjoying this type of trip. With most of the horse handling done by the guys, and the cooking done by Calvin, she had time to relax and pitch in wherever needed. Dinkey was also thoroughly enjoying herself, since she just had to follow Deb around, and seemed to be getting extra petting. Yep, he could just see the grins on both their faces.

Fly fishing was always available, so whenever time allowed, Clyde and Pablo would wander off to the nearest stream or lake. Practicing casting was the most fun. Getting a fish on the hook was the icing on the cake. They were always gently removed from the barbless hooks and returned to their watery world, followed by a respectful salute from the catcher.

After the study group came back to camp in the early evening and had dinner, they always went off by themselves to huddle and have their discussions. Pablo thought this odd and asked Clyde about it. Clyde responded, "It seems they had a preconceived idea the packers would hang around and try to argue with their discussion and summations. This is why they wanted to go solely on their own. I was able to convince them it would not happen with us. I told them they would be free to conduct their discussions without our interference after a great dinner. So, let's just give it time and see how this works out. I feel it's human nature to be open to outside discussion and input if they don't feel threatened. Give it time and watch what happens."

By the third night, Pablo was astonished to hear the leader tell us four we were welcome to listen in as that evening's discussion was going to take place under the overhead tarp near the campfire. It was getting colder and maybe this had something to do with it. The four just sat quietly and listened to the chatter. Dr. Wise, Deb, and Clyde all were patient, as the topics where nothing they hadn't heard about before. One of the issues discussed was having horses around main creek areas or lakes. Clyde just smiled. This caught the attention of the hydrologist member of the group, who asked, "Clyde, what are your thoughts?"

"Well," he began, "before you folks got back today, all the horses were turned out right here next to camp to go free graze. Look around, you don't see a single horse. They were watered before we came up here and stopped. After being unsaddled, all they wanted to do was eat. That's their nature. The grasses along the water edges are more of the reed variety and a little on the coarse side for their mouths. They like the bunch grasses up on the hillsides. Sure, they will hang around for about twenty minutes until all their buddies are freed, then they gently start hopping for the higher hillsides where the more tender grass is. This is learned behavior, as they have been here many times. There are numerous small springs up in the trees on the mountainsides, so no need to come down here to the main bodies of water. Also, they know, up there are far less bugs to bother them as the evening comes. And it's warmer too.

"All night, they'll stay up there eating and sleeping. They'll move around a little but not much. In the morning you won't see 'em either, but don't panic, I know where they hang out. Most of the time I have 'em back here in fifteen minutes. When they stay up there on the high and dry, minimal to no environmental damage occurs. The last place they want to hang out is in the wet riparian zones. You wouldn't want to either if you were out there.

"To do this takes time and patience, but the older ones teach the younger ones. The horses will tell you if they like the area. If not, they find a new spot. Most commercial packers, private horse folks, and even USFS packers think they have to have complete, minute-by-minute control of the animals. This is why they tend to tie 'em up all night. This can lead to serious resource damage and, I feel, is not kind to the animals. They typically don't get enough to eat and after a long trek will lose weight. Every hour they are on the trail, they need at least that in eating time. So just let 'em hobble free and eat and rest when they want. This only works if the animals are comfortable in the high country. If they come up from the flatlands and get spooked at night, that's when the private folks find their animals back at the trailheads the next day. There is no substitute for well-trained mountain horses. Their lives, and mine as well, are so much easier. In the forty years plus I've been doing this, I've never once had my animals leave me."

Pablo could see by the expression on the faces that this was sobering new information to the group. Apparently the group hadn't heard this type of viewpoint before, or had ever cared to listen. Disbelief was written on all their faces.

The next morning proved interesting. Upon rising, while during coffee, Pablo could hear the group's quiet discussion about not see-ing or hearing the bells of a single horse. They were almost in group satisfaction with the possibility Clyde may have to eat his words. Clyde never said a word, just winked at Pablo and motioned for him to gather an armful of lead ropes and follow. The duo headed up the mountain and disappeared into the forest. Within fifteen minutes, the ears of Dog perked up and the sound of the bells were soon after heard by the group. In they came, all seventeen in single file, being led in two groups. They were then calmly separated and tied up, ready for saddling. After viewing this, the quiet group fin-ished the last of the morning breakfast, put on their day packs after loading their lunches, and proceeded off to the day's work.

With the workday in front of them, Clyde's company all agreed no rush was in order. Calmly the horses were saddled and the camp was broken down and made ready for loading. By then it was such a well-oiled routine that few words were needed and the task was completed within one and a half hours. And then the procession was on its way.

This went on for several days, as they headed generally eastward, including the areas of Bench Valley and Blackcap Basin, and then rounding back first to the south and then westward toward Crown Pass and the Crown Lake area. The group had stopped for a moment by Halfmoon Lake, which has a most beautiful backdrop of granite cliffs, like something straight out of a postcard. With a near-perfect view, it was with regret that, due to the lack of grazing for the stock, no camping was to take place there, so they moved on.

At Crown Lake, just after camp was set up, a huge thunder storm came in and dumped rain by the buckets. Fortunately, it was to be a two-day stopover, so the group just had to dig in and wait it out. Not only was thunder blasting, but lightning came down all around and sometimes landed scarily close. The horses never flinched from their grazing and neither did Clyde, Deb, or Dr. Wise. Dinkey was fine, but Dog initially was jumping out of his skin, although the reassuring hand of Calvin eventually calmed him down. Pablo was the one who never really got used to the blasting and woke up often during the night, wondering if it was going to be his last.

With no traveling on the schedule for the next day, and the USFS group out doing their work, Deb, Clyde, and Dinkey went off for a walk toward Scepter Lake. Calvin and Dog were content to just lie around camp. Pablo decided today was a good day to get out his fishing pole. Off he went toward the inlet side of Crown Lake. He had always heard this lake held the largest fish in the area. With over one hundred lakes here, that was saying something.

The inlet end of the lake was fed from the creek that came from around the backside of the land peninsula and was flat and full of meadow grass and border reeds. Perfect ground for fish food generation, emptying right at his feet. He carefully tied on a Black Gnat fly at the end of his leader and slowly started fly casting motions out on the gently swirling confluence of the emptying stream and the stillness of the flat lake. He was able to get several fake casts out, thus allowing ample line be fed out to get the distance he desired. With a gentle set down of the fly in perfect unison with the touchdown of the leader line, all was calm for a few seconds. The gently rotating fly caused small ripples in a 360 degree direction.

Suddenly, *wham*, the biggest trout Pablo had ever seen broke the surface with the fly attached and presented a perfect profile, with sunlight reflecting off this beautiful rainbow trout. It slammed his fly rod down so hard that Pablo panicked and let out line from his reel, afraid he would break the two-pound leader line and lose his prize. Whenever the trout swam toward him, he would crank the reel to take back in the line, only to have Mr. Trout turn and make a run for deeper water, forcing him to quickly let back out the line he had just retrieved. This went on over and over, but he was making small gains each time. After what seemed like an hour, but was only about ten minutes, the fish began to tire. In came the fish, breaking the surface often and giving Pablo a scare, as he knew this is when most fish got unhooked. In he came, only to make a break for it. Then the process started over. Since trout have soft mouths, Pablo knew any moment this wonder of the high country lakes could shake the hook loose.

Eventually, he drew the tiring fish within four feet of the shore. That's when Pablo paused and got his handheld fishnet out. With the rod in his raised left hand and arm and the net in his outstretched right hand, he gently led the fish in, with its head tilted slightly up, and scooped the net under to finally capture this wonderment of the lake. Up on the grassy bank he placed the fish and removed the netting. There to his amazement was a twenty-two-inch, two-pound rainbow trout. Not just the biggest he had ever caught, but the biggest he had ever seen. After a long pause for reverence, Pablo cleaned the trout and proudly carried it back to camp. He was done fishing for the day, completely absorbed by this single experience.

After pictures were taken, Calvin started to prepare Pablo's prize as an addition to the main dinner course. His method was real simple: just season the fish with salt, pepper, and juice squeezed from a lemon, wrap it in foil, and slowly cook it over the open fire grate.

That evening, during dinner, all enjoyed the fish addition to the menu. With smiles and congratulations, Pablo somehow felt more connected to the group. This sense of connection had been slowly growing the whole trip, but now it was more noticeable. He felt whenever groups break bread together, something happens that brings the people together. The conversation gravitated to the trails, lakes, and practices of commercial packers. He was beginning to realize there was far more common ground than originally thought. The group saw that with careful, well-thought-out stock practices by packers, much good was obtained. Both the packers and the specialists valued the nonmechanical approach of wilderness management, up to a point. If safety was a concern, then a limited amount of mechanical intervention was necessary. This would include addressing a suspended tree on a dangerous fall zone or a trail route where some blasting would be necessary to stabilize the upslope and downslope, work which, if done right, would maintain safety for generations.

Pablo sincerely felt that a meeting of the minds had occurred by the end of this trip. The commercial livestock packers, the various USFS specialists, and those representing environmental groups all can come together in the Sierra high country and work out their differences. Yep, it's true, if John Muir and President Roosevelt could do it, then so could we modern folks. Breaking bread together numerous times seems to have had that effect, and Pablo couldn't help but feel he had played a major part in this whole phenomenon. For, after all, it was his prized trout that was the focus of attention on their last meal together.

CHAPTER 10

The Creek Fire

On a balmy early September afternoon, the sky was perfectly clear. It was one of those days just right for lounging out on a chair under the pine trees and enjoying the wonders of the forest. Business at the other location at Dinkey Creek, where only hour rides were done, was getting slower due to a hot spell. When there was an open day on the pack trip schedule, Pablo would often go down to Clyde's Dinkey Creek station and relieve that rider so she could enjoy a day off. He had been busy all morning this particular day, but as it got warmer, the rides tapered off. Since he couldn't leave, this was the time Pablo usually dove into a favorite book and relaxed. He was reading about the early native American Indians of California. He knew they were related to the Mexican Indians of his native land, and was enjoying learning about the similarities.

About 3:00 in the afternoon, he looked up and noticed a modest cloud just visible over the mountaintops to the northwest. Not noticing any other clouds and knowing no rain was in the forecast, he thought it strange, but got back into his book.

After another hour, he looked up and saw that this cloud had developed into a huge, anvil-shaped, thunder-type cloud. But he thought it strange that there was no wind, no other clouds, and the temperature was still warm. Usually there is a rapid cool down with summer storms. What really grabbed his attention was the center-mass, rolling nature of this darkening cloud.

Just about then, the radio came to life talking about a fire over in the Big Creek area. It was described as small, only a few acres, and containment was felt assured as the Forest Service was doing a wait and watch approach. Pablo then realized this phenomenon of nature was no cloud at all but a smoke plume from an extremely hot source. He knew the forest in this region had been a victim of at least eighty years of overly aggressive fire suppression by the Forest Service, especially after WW2, when hundreds of experienced bomber pilots were available to drop fire retardment and bigger and better dozers became more readily available. Clyde had told him how, after fires, the Forest Service would replant a burned area with just a single species of tree, mostly Jeffery pines, since they had fast regrowing potential and thus better market value. Even he noticed this didn't fit with nature's plan, since the natural ecosystem contained a wide variety of tree species. These new trees were planted in high density, so it was no surprise that in hot, dry, and windy summers explosive fires would result, fires that were so hot they killed everything standing.

From his readings, Pablo knew that for thousands of years the Indians would commonly set fires to clear out the underbrush and small trees. They did this for several reasons. In the lowlands, this practice resulted in fewer but larger oak trees. From these they knew they would get a bumper crop of acorns that were free of worms. If they allowed the area to remain choked with smaller trees, all competing for the same amount of water and nutrients, the net result would be a poor crop of nuts.

In the higher elevations, they typically would burn a five- to ten-acre area. This was done in the late fall and would allow for the abundant spring regrowth of browse, necessary for the deer. This created a perfect hunting situation for the native people. Pablo knew the bands of Indians lived in extended family groups and had territories of eight to twenty miles square. However, they easily moved to a new location when needed. Lightning caused most of the forest fires, and the Indians certainly didn't have the means to put them out. So they simply moved out of the way and came back to the area the following year. Those fires were usually self-limiting to a few hundred acres, so no major destruction was caused. Pablo was amazed to learn that this approach to living with and tending to the environment worked so well throughout the state that California had the densest population of Native Americans in the whole United States. And through all these thousands of years, they never overharvested any resource, or polluted a single stream, or put any petroleum particulates in the sky. They were so in balance with nature that they could have easily continued in this fashion for millennia. It never ceased to amaze Pablo the impact outside immigration has had on the land, water, and air in only the last 150 years.

Pablo's gaze left the strange cloud formation and returned to his Native American reading. He was quickly absorbed in the food preparation methods used for thousands of years before outside settlers arrived on the scene. He discovered the multiple bulbs within the plants of the area here and in lower elevations, and was especially fascinated by those from the Mariposa lily and the brodiaea (blue dick). The natives dug them up with digging sticks. These wooden sticks, sharpened at one end, were three to four feet long. The extracted bulbs were usually baked in a small pit, no more than two-feet deep and lined with rocks. A fire was built over the rocks to heat them. With the ashes and coals removed, the hot rocks were lined with leaves. The bulbs were then placed over the leaves and covered with more leaves, the topsoil was replaced, and the whole project was left for about thirty minutes. After that, the toasty bulbs were ready to eat. The Indians cooked multiple types of vegetables in these earthen ovens.

Other times, the plants were placed in watertight, tightly woven baskets that were partially filled with water. Then hot rocks were placed inside. The rocks were gently stirred to keep them from burning a hole in the basket. Soon enough, the cooked vegetables were ready to eat or to be dried and stored for winter, when they could be rehydrated and warmed to eat.

The acorn process fascinated Pablo. These were abundant, and were the main staple of the local Indians' diet. The acorns were stored initially in granaries, which were poles placed upright in a circle and tied together with buck brush or vines. Additional brush was placed inside the granary to discourage rodents from invading. Acorns were generally gathered in the fall, cracked like a walnut, and dried. This usually only took a few days, after which the acorns were placed in mortar holes and pounded with rock pestles. Pablo had often observed mortar holes in the area, usually clustered in small groups. He concluded that multiple women must have sat together and worked at the same time. He paused for a moment with a smile. Considering the length of time it took for the whole process, these must have been lengthy gossip sessions. He remembered the obsidian chip mining zones Clyde had shown him before. That job was mostly a male occupation. Pablo noted they were always far away from the grinding holes, and realized the men must have wanted to keep their distance. Some things never change.

After the pulverized acorns were removed from the mortar holes, they were placed in a small depression lined with leaves. The nut powder was no more than two inches thick when warm water was poured over the mesh repeatedly. This was done to leach out the tannic acid. The process usually took about thirty minutes. Sometimes they would put four to five inches of acorn meal into a watertight basket, where it was thinned with water and heated with hot rocks. It would then be gently placed in cool water to gel, making it suitable for use as acorn bread.

The men did their part in obtaining meat. The Indians ate mostly deer, squirrel, rabbits, and whatever else they could get. Hunting was usually done with bow and arrow, but snares were used for the smaller game. The meat was either barbecued if for immediate consumption, or jerked for winter storage.

Obviously, they never knew what a grocery store was, but for thousands of years, everything they needed could be obtained from nature. With no written language, wisdom, passed down verbally from generation to generation, was the link.

This was also true with the medicinal plants. The Indians didn't know about the plants' chemical ingredients or how they worked, but word of mouth from the elders was gospel. Leaves or stems were usually rendered into the form of teas, poultices, or washes. For instance, bearclover (also known as mountain misery) leaves were used as a tea for coughs or colds. Buckeye leaves were used in a tea that treated lung congestion. The seeds were crushed and used as a poultice for hemorrhoids. However, they did know the nuts from the buckeye were poisonous.

There was also golden fleece, whose roots were pulverized and drunk as a tea or applied topically. The top part of the flower was

California Gray Squirrel

used for the tea, which was used to induce abortion, mainly during the first month of pregnancy. Manzanita leaf, when placed in the mouth, increased saliva and acted as a thirst quencher. The berries would be mashed, soaked in water, and then strained to make a sweet cider. When used as a topical wash, the berries were good for treating poison oak. Mistletoe leaves were boiled and drunk as a tea for rheumatism. But, mistletoe berries are poisonous and never used.

Penstemon leaves were boiled and drunk as a tea for tuberculosis and bad colds. They could also be used as a wash to soothe pain from burns and to promote new skin growth. Pennyroyal flowers and stems were boiled and drunk for colds, fevers, and morning sickness for pregnant women. The flower was often rubbed on the skin to repel mosquitos. Western chokecherry bark was stripped and boiled. It was used as a gargle to treat hoarseness. It was also used by speakers and singers to improve their voices. The pits of wild cherries are poisonous, as well as the cherries themselves when they are green. Yarrow applied to cuts and sores promoted healing. Liquefied, it could be used as an eye wash to eliminate redness. It could also be drunk on a regular basis to sharpen the memory. The soaproot bulb's soap-like substance could be rubbed on the scalp to combat baldness.

Again, the Native Americans didn't know the chemical components of these plants nor their mechanisms of action, simply that they worked. Many natives felt, even after the influx of pharmacies, their traditional natural remedies worked best. They never would dream to overharvest or try to change the flora or fauna in any way, as nature exists in the way the creators intended. Never did they pollute the air or water. By taking only what nature gave them, and using it in the best possible way, they maintained their prosperity for thousands of years.

Pablo took a pause, sat the book upon his lap, closed his eyes, and let that sink in. He felt a strong sense of comfort, even relaxation, knowing the Indians' environment was the same he was sitting in at the moment. He started to become conscious of the impact on their world by immigration over the last 150 years, and how the environment had been treated during that short time because of attempts to modify it to the needs of man, instead of man conforming to nature.

Upon opening his eyes, he was startled by the glaring vision of the anvil-like cloud formation floating before him to the northwest. It appeared the firestorm from that forest fire was getting out of control. He turned on the radio to listen to the Forest Service chatter and was shocked to find out the small, two-acre fire from the afternoon before had blown up. The huge amounts of fuel load on the ground—some said it was twenty times the normal amount—combined with over ten times the historical tree density per acre due to no logging and overactive fire suppression, had created a prescription for disaster. Once again, human attempts to control the environment had resulted in disaster. There was no better evidence of that than the scary pillar of smoke in the distance. In fact, this looked like a true firestorm, a phenomenon he had read about in one of his college classes. He had learned that firestorms resulted from the surrounding air being drawn into the center of the fire. The influx of oxygen caused the heat to rapidly rise, something called the stack effect. With the strong wind—which he could detect from the swaying tops of the pine trees—interacting with the blowing embers, Pablo knew big trouble was in the making.

It didn't take long for the anvil formation to double in size and drift to the east just north of him. He knew the buoyancy of the rising heat would put flaming debris far downwind and start numerous spot fires in its path. If this continued, he knew nothing could stop this horrific stampede of flames. With countless acres of heavy, dry fuel load that had built up over the past seventy-five or so years, a catastrophic fire was inevitable.

Pablo looked back down at his book describing the Native American way of life for thousands of years and, seeing what was unfolding in the sky, a small tear appeared in his eyes as he realized the contrast.

Dropping the book, he ran to the landline telephone and called Clyde up at the Wishon Station. Clyde had known about the fire but couldn't determine the magnitude since he didn't have the view that Pablo had. With Pablo's new information, and after viewing the fire line the Forest Services had forwarded to his computer, he knew this wasn't going to be a simple put-out. He had heard from the chatter that afternoon and the evening prior that it was declared contained to a couple of acres and that the USFS had released three pumper units for the evening. By morning the whole situation had changed. An explosion is the best way to describe it. Since the fire was over twenty miles away and tracking to the north by northeast, he advised Pablo to sit tight and keep a close vigil and let him know if the wind shifted toward him.

From hearing the radio traffic and viewing the computer updates forwarded to him, Clyde knew the USFS was in all-out panic mode. They were calling for all hands on deck, looking for outside agency help, and seeking air support as well. With the numerous other fires going on in the state, he knew outside help would be in short supply. Roads and prior old fire lines were useless. With the windblown flames jumping from treetop to treetop (known as crowning), and the thick understory fueling the inferno, temperatures would exceed 2,000 degrees. Enough to melt metal.

With only a glance at the road map, it was clear only one road was available for the people to get in or out of the Edison, Florence, and Mammoth Pool areas. But the flames were rapidly overtaking that route and thus those people were likely already trapped. Their only hope was to abandon their camps and vehicles and all—men, women, and children—wade into the lakes. The larger the body of water the better. With the updrafts, the oxygen throughout the forest was being sucked upward, but hopefully this phenomenon would be lessened over large bodies of water and leave enough O2 for the people to survive. With cell service knocked out, no one knew at this early stage if they had taken those measures. But soon, to Clyde's relief, satellite calls started coming in and apparently the trapped people were doing just that. With the flames totally over-taking the road, the only option to get them out was by helicopter. With the smoke putting visibility down to zero, initially this was not an option.

People safety was one issue; the other was the encircled live-stock. With the roads blocked and authorities dealing with higher priority evacuation requirements, the ranchers and horsepackers were not allowed to gather and evacuate their animals. Clyde knew each rancher's allotment areas that were being engulfed and got sickened by what devastation was happening to those poor ani-mals, as well as to the wild animals in those stricken areas. Even if the cattle, deer, bears, and so on were to get lucky and find a location that allowed the flames to go around them, trying to walk through hot ash beds was just as deadly as being engulfed by flame. Within a few steps their hoofs would start to melt. They might survive the walk through the fire line, but would soon be so lame that they would lie down and never get back up, soon to die. As Clyde learned soon after the ordeal ended, some ranchers suffered 100 percent livestock loss from the fire itself, while others had to euthanize over 80 percent of their herds afterward.

The pack station at Edison Lake was doing evasive measures to save their horses and mules. With sat phone relays, Clyde knew they were lining the animals out in strings and heading east up into the Sierra high country, where there was far less fire danger and the chances of survival were much better. This turned out to be a smart move. The horses of one unfortunate cattle operator named Wagner were simply trapped. Their eastward route was blocked by the flames. Yet after two days of fire all around them, the horses had miraculously survived. But with the haystacks burned and the ground charred, there was nothing left for them to eat. Fortunately, the horses were confined in steel corrals and thus were prevented from escaping to the burn areas, where their feet would have surely been damaged beyond repair.

As the radio chatter and computer graphs continued, Clyde noticed an all-too-frequent phenomenon occurring. He had read about this often, something first noticed in old war stories. During battle, when things get desperate, it's amazing who does and doesn't rise to the leadership level in a positive way. This is why so many of the Metal of Honor recipients were from the lesser or even bottom ranks. No one knows their true inner character and strength until put to the test. Also, interesting to note, was how often those in leadership roles who were expected to lead were nowhere to be found. They basically hid under their desks and waited for the crisis to blow over. This was happening again now. The calls for Forest Service personnel to led convoys of cattlemen and their rigs through the fire line to evacuate the animals went initially unanswered. The ones who volunteered where those of the lower ranks, for whom this type of duty was way outside their job description.

Among these was Deborah McDougald, who oversaw the pack station permittees for the Forest Service and whose job had nothing to do with the cattlemen. Another was Tony Bonelli, who works in the Forest Service with the OHV (Off-Highway Vehicle) unit. And there was also Phil Lodge, a Fresno County deputy sheriff. None of these individuals were required to perform this task, but volunteered because of the urgent need. And they did it over and over, evacuating the cattlemen and their stock through the fire, some doing so daily for a week or more straight. The employees responsible for the oversight and well-being of the cattlemen seemed to be MIA. This was odd but, unfortunately, not unusual.

As the fire raged on, the horses owned by cattlewoman Emily Wagner were going without feed. A lower-level Forest Service employee who was tasked with bringing in supplies for the firefighters learned about the desperate situation of Wagner's horses. He loaded up the remaining room in his flatbed truck with hay and asked a Forest Service fire pumper truck to follow him in through the burning area for the emergency delivery. The flames were raging so bad on both sides of the road that twice he had to stop and let

Debbie McDougald

the pumper truck put out the flames on the hay. He arrived safely with all the hay and supplies. The trapped people in the lakes were airlifted by Chinook helicopter after the smoke cleared enough. All arrived safe.

By the end of the Creek Fire, over 350 thousand acres were burned and over $350 million of public money was spent. The fire, California's largest ever at the time, burned about 180 structures, including homes. Fortunately, no human lives were lost. The domestic livestock didn't fare as well. As mentioned, many cattle operations suffered a 100 percent loss of their animals, and also had their cow camps burned to the ground. Even aluminum trailers were reduced to mere puddles of melted metal. Wildlife habitat loss was clearly enormous, but no one has calculated the loss of wild animal and plant life.

As one looks out over the burned areas today, all one can see is a charred, desolate landscape with blackened sticks reaching skyward like tombstone markers. They too, within ten to fifteen years, will fall to their final resting places. Some pockets survived better than others and will serve as seed sources for regeneration. But, this will take seventy-five to one hundred years. Even then, this will only happen if smaller fires are repeatedly allowed to clear the emerging underbrush every ten to twenty years. If such fires are aggressively put out, then again, as with previous policy, the undergrowth will choke out the much-needed sunlight for the new trees to reach maturity. Hillsides full of dense, brush will develop, just waiting for the next catastrophic fire. The Creek Fire was the product of a modern, man-made disaster that only took about seventy-five years to create. Too bad we couldn't learn from the original human inhabitants, who had been here, some say, for over 20,000 years.

As the fire raged on, Pablo, Deb, and Clyde had to make plans. Even though the fire was a considerable distance from them, at any time winds could change, and so could their situation. The whole Sierra National Forest was declared closed. Since the fire started over the Labor Day weekend, Clyde's Dinkey station was about to close up for the season anyway. Pack trips into the John Muir Wilderness were stopped and all the campgrounds were closed. This led to a complete evacuation of most all humans in the area. The only remaining people were Pablo, Bill, Deb, and Clyde, along with cattle operators Mary Piasecki and Dennis Atkinson on the east side of Wishon Lake and five PG&E personnel.

The horses from Dinkey were moved to the Wishon headquarters, where there was plenty of hay and water, and no imminent danger from the fire, which was still over twenty miles away as the crow flies. The four decided it would be wise to gather all the cattle and place them in the holding pasture. In this fence-enclosed, eighty-acre meadow, the cattle would have the best chance for survival in the event the fire overran the area. Hopefully it would go around and not burn the open meadow itself. The horses could also be placed there if needed. In addition, they moved extra portable corral panels to the open Wishon Lake shoreline as an alternative location. With all this preparation, it was also agreed that the PG&E folks, Mary and Dennis, and the four members of Clyde's crew would dive into the access tunnel of the Helms Power House if the worse happened and there was a complete fire engulfment. The obvious hope was that that would never be necessary, and, as things turned out, it never was.

The process of gathering the cattle was unlike anything Pablo had ever experienced. Most of the time the smoke was completely clouding the whole area like a thick fog. The smell was like standing next to a campfire with the smoke blowing in your face and never moving out of the way. Your eyes burned and you always had a slight cough. Pushing cattle down the main McKinley Grove road on the opening day of deer season was something that was never done. The traffic was always horrendous and thus more trouble then it was worth. This time, the cattle were led down the road with not a vehicle in sight. No sound, just quiet and choking smoke. It was almost spooky, as if a major apocalypse had occurred and they were the only ones remaining. Gradually, over several days, all the cattle were gathered and deposited in the safer open meadow enclosure. With plenty of food supplies, all that was left was to wait it out.

As the fire enlarged it started to make its way toward the town of Shaver Lake. With about 1,000 inhabitants and hundreds of homes, this had the potential for serious private property damage and human loss. The Shaver area is about 20,000 acres of private land held by the Southern California Edison company (SCE). This island of forest land is managed by them and with a totally different philosophy than the Forest Service. Led for thirty years by lead forester John Mount, their policy is one of intermittent thinning followed by controlled burns, a stark contrast to the Forest Service pattern of totally shutting down of all logging and controlled burns.

As the fire approached Shaver's outside boundaries, it was feared the town would be lost. But then the fire started to "lay down."This means it went from a rapid tree-to-tree movement pattern to a slow, groundhugging, far less intense burning that could be controlled more easily. And due to SCE's forest management practices, there was so much less fuel load on the ground that in many places the fire simply went out on its own. In other places, backfires were attempted along the lines, but these fires couldn't maintain themselves and thus just went out. As the days progressed, the computer maps showed the outline of the fire's progression and it was clear the fire was going around the SCE land and the town of Shaver. Afterward, a clear picture of a horseshoe pattern around the properly managed SCE forest was a testimony to the years of John Mount's sound forest management practices. In the end, nothing in the town of Shaver burned.

After helping the Clydes with the gathering of the cattle for safer keeping in Hall Meadow, Pablo was returned to class at Fresno State. Once he went down the hill, road blocks would not permit his returning back up. Even after going down the mountain and out of the fire line, Pablo still had to contend with the choking smoke in the San Joaquin Valley floor. He could only wait and wonder if Deb, Bill, Clyde, Dinkey, and Patsy were doing OK. Since the forest had been shut down, no new pack trips were allowed to start. However, there will still groups that had been out in the wilderness prior to the shutdown.

Clyde spent his time retrieving these groups, one by one, as their return dates came up. He knew they were well out of harm's way, since the fire line was over twenty miles away and they were camped above the 10,000 foot level, where the fuel load was minimal. Additionally the wind direction was such that they mostly had clear blue skies above.

Finally the last group's return date came up. They had been tucked away in the wilderness high above the tree line. For the past five days a frantic family member living in Southern California was hounding Clyde with multiple daily calls about having to rescue the group. Even though he was given repeated assurances of their safety, the caller remained persistent. Clyde kept a cool head and maintained professionalism on the phone. But each time, when he hung up, Deb could hear soft curse words from her husband. He explained to her that on the last phone call, the caller stated he, himself, was going to drive up and "rescue" his family group. That explained why Deb overheard her husband say, "Go ahead, you will be met by the Sheriff's office and CHP and be told to turn around. If you don't, then enjoy your time being handcuffed in the back of a patrol car while you get a free taxi ride to the county jail." The caller had slammed the phone down in response.

The next morning, as per schedule, Clyde had the horses saddled and was heading up the trail. Upon reaching the group four hours later, they had just finished packing their gear and welcomed him. There was only a slight amount of smoke in the high atmosphere that day, which prompted the leader to ask, "Is there a fire somewhere? We just noticed the smoke this morning." "Yep," Clyde responded. "It's still a long ways away, but it's about time for you guys to bug out anyway. No problem getting you to your cars, but you'll be going down an alternate route since the highway through the town of Shaver is closed." They replied, "No problem, we're glad you didn't come early and force us to leave. Had a great time and the fishing was unbelievable."

Out they went, and when all the gear was back in their cars and the group was ready to roll, Clyde radioed the US Forest Service law enforcement and an escort out was arranged. They were instructed to call the pack station when they reached the valley floor, which they did. All made it home safely.

After about three weeks, roads were reopened and the Forest Service gave the OK to load all the cattle trucks and head down the mountain. This was done all in one day, with Pablo coming up for the weekend to lend a hand. A convoy of trucks was loaded and headed down the mountain to the winter ranch pastures, being followed by the numerous gooseneck trailers loaded with horses. It was quite a procession.

Since the fire never got to Pablo's section of the Sierra National Forest, his heading up the mountain with the Clydes earlier in the day to retrieve the stock had been his first sight of the destruction. Smoke was still curling up on both sides of the road. Complete devastation surrounded him. The shock of the formerly pristine forest's ruin was overwhelming. Clyde told Pablo, "Don't look away. Keep staring and remember this your whole life. With the USFS's policy of kicking the can down the road for someone else to deal with and letting the problem compound on itself, this is a perfect example of poor planning always leading to poor results. You can apply this lesson to anything you encounter your whole life. Doing the right thing is always the right thing to do. No matter how inconvenient."

The aftermath of the evacuation was filled with numerous return trips by Clyde and Deb. The occasional stray cattle were located and gathered into the corral and ready to be hauled down. The final closing down of the buildings for the winter took place. This process included draining all water lines, covering all windows, removing the portable horse corral panels, and properly storing all water troughs and tanks. With the last exit for the fall season, there was always the customary silent salute to the station and the whispering of "Have a good sleep. See ya in the spring. You survived another year."

All this was on Pablo's daydreaming mind for a moment while in chemistry class. He snapped to and reminded himself, "Time to stay on task. SCHOOL."

Index

About the Author

Deb and Allen Clyde. *Photo courtesy of C. Howard Stimmel.*

Dr. Allen Clyde has operated a horse-packing service in the John Muir Wilderness for forty years, transporting over twenty thousand visitors and their supplies. He is also a podiatric physician and surgeon. Dr. Clyde has served on the Fresno County (California) Board of Education for nearly twenty years. He lives in Clovis, California. *Trail Talk* is his second book. His first book, *Life Lessons on the Sierra Trail*, was published in 2020.

About Claudia Fletcher

Claudia Fletcher. *Photo courtesy of Claudia Fletcher.*

Professional artist and muralist **Claudia Fletcher,** born and raised on a cotton and alfalfa farm in Madera, California, possessed an inherent love for the San Joaquin Valley and a natural talent for capturing its essence through art. Following in the footsteps of her artist grandmother, Fletcher was only eight years old when she participated in her first art show.

She won many art competitions; produced commissioned artwork, portrait paintings, and drawings for clients across the United States; and created murals for several cities. She also painted the official poster for the annual Clovis Rodeo. Referring to her favorite art subject, Fletcher said, "The power and magnificence of the horse was my first channel for the expression of my talent in drawing and painting."

About Diane Breuer

Diane Breuer. *Photo courtesy of Diane Breuer.*

Diane Sauble Breuer was born in Los Angeles, CA. She studied art at the University of Art in Madras and Calcutta, Batik Study at the artist's colony in Cholamandal, India, and at Fresno State. She loves pastel but also paints in oils, acrylics, watercolor, pen and ink, and clay. She has won numerous awards including. Her artwork was also used on the cover of the book *Alley Cat at the Mercy of the Gods*.

Diane is a signature member of PSWC, ACA, and SWA. She served on the SWA and ACA boards as publicity chair, newsletter chair, webmaster, vice president, and president. She is on the Pastel Society of the West Coast board as webmaster. Diane owned the Fresno Art Hub, a fine art gallery and studio, where over thirty artists had work on display. Now retired from the gallery, she continues giving demonstrations and workshops. She works from her studio located on her property in Fresno County.

You may see Diane's artwork at www.dianebreuer.com.

www.ingramcontent.com/pod-product-compliance
Lightning Source LLC
Chambersburg PA
CBHW021153130626
46554CB00005B/1799